SELECTING ETHNOGRAPHIC INFORMANTS

SO-AZT-472

JEFFREY C. JOHNSON
East Carolina University

Qualitative Research Methods
Volume 22

SAGE Publications
International Educational and Professional Publisher
Newbury Park London New Delhi

For information address:

SAGE Publications, Inc.
2455 Teller Road
Newbury Park, California 91320
E-mail: order@sagepub.com

SAGE Publications Ltd.
6 Bonhill Street
London EC2A 4PU
United Kingdom

SAGE Publications India Pvt. Ltd.
M-32 Market
Greater Kailash I
New Delhi 110 048 India

Printed in the United States of America

Library of Congress Cataloging-in-Publication Data

Johnson, Jeffrey C.
    Selecting ethnographic informants / by Jeffrey C. Johnson.
        p.   cm. — (Qualitative research methods ; v. 22)
    Includes bibliographical references.
    ISBN 0-8039-3586-2. — ISBN 0-8039-3587-0 (pbk.)
    1. Interviewing in ethnology. 2. Ethnology—Field work.
    I. Title. II. Series.
    GN346.3.J64 1990
305.8'00723—dc20   90-43951
                                                                            CIP

95 96 97 98 99 10 9 8 7 6 5 4 3 2

Production Editor: Susan McElroy

CONTENTS

EDITORS' INTRODUCTION

One of the reasons qualitative research has established niches in such a broad range of academic disciplines can be traced to the fortunate fact that people will talk about their lives not only with family and friends, but with professional strangers. Successful qualitative research hinges on bonds linking the observer and those observed. The nature of these ties depends, of course, on which data recovery techniques are utilized. When social surveys are involved, researchers engage "respondents" in relationships that are relatively short-lived and emotionally inconsequential for both parties. When study designs call for sustained participant observation, these relationships expand and develop their own histories. Classic ethnographies — whether concerning societies of the traditional or street-corner variety — attest to the ethnographer's debt to "key informants," "translators," and other locals for diverse contributions to the research effort. Yet, too often the qualitative research record is vague about how informants came to volunteer or contract for their services. Indeed, part of the mystique of fieldwork emanates from the incredible good luck ethnographers seem to have in finding knowledgeable, responsible, amiable informants.

In *Selecting Ethnographic Informants*, Volume 22 of Sage's Qualitative Research Methods Series, Jeffrey C. Johnson contends that it is not enough for contemporary researchers to know how to get information from informants, or even how to get along with them. Today, the standard of reliability compels us to know in addition precisely how informants fit with their own culture. Accordingly, this book presents procedures for informant selection where ethnographers need to know the informant's structural position in a social network, functional role in an organization, or level of competence in a field of knowledge.

Johnson advances two frameworks for choosing informants. With a *theory-driven* approach, the researcher begins by deciding in advance which statuses and cultural abilities potential informants must have. With a *data-driven* approach, the researcher first explores and then formally analyzes networks (for example, via multidimensional scaling or factor analysis) to discover the social leverage of candidate informants. In the application of

5

either framework, the idea is to deal with issues of personality, empathy, availability, and special personal attributes in the second step of the search. With this sequence, Johnson prepares us for the temptation of settling for informants who meet the rapport requirement but who are simply not as well qualified as others for the research question.

Over the last several decades, advances in qualitative research have improved data collection and analyses, as well as the writing of ethnographies. Properly, Johnson has now extended methodological reflection to aspects of informant recruitment. Keenly aware of how the "garbage in, garbage out" syndrome wreaks havoc with the best theoretical insights, Johnson provides a balanced strategy for sampling ethnographic informants. Forewarned is forearmed.

— Marc L. Miller
Peter K. Manning
John Van Maanen

ACKNOWLEDGMENTS

Some of the work reported in this volume has been supported by the University of North Carolina Sea Grant College Program under grants NA83-AA-d-00012, NA85AA-d-SG022, and NA86AA-d-SG046. Funding provided by Office of Sea Grant and the National Marine Fisheries Service, NOAA, U.S. Department of Commerce.

I would like to thank John Van Maanen, Peter Manning, Jerome Kirk, Susan Weller, David Griffith, and Marc Miller for their helpful comments. Finally, I would particularly like to thank Kay Evans for her patience and help in producing this volume.

SELECTING ETHNOGRAPHIC INFORMANTS

JEFFREY C. JOHNSON
East Carolina University

1. THAT WHICH IS EXPLICIT IN ETHNOGRAPHY

Definitions

In the lead paragraph to the *Professional Stranger*, Michael Agar (1980) informs us that his book concerns the collaboration between social researcher and those being studied. The main purpose of such a collaborative relationship is the exchange of information, and it is that relationship — "fortuitously encountered or consciously constructed — that constitute[s] the core of ethnographic fieldwork" (p. 1). Whether one agrees with Agar's view of ethnographic fieldwork or not, it is certainly the case that the people an ethnographer studies are an invaluable source of data. This addition to the Qualitative Research Methods Series, as the title suggests, will focus on the underlying concerns surrounding the *conscious* construction of these collaborative relationships, particularly as they relate to the nature of information being exchanged. This book focuses on a single aspect of the overall ethnographic enterprise, an aspect referred to by Kirk and Miller (1986) as "scoring a chance," that constitutes the logistics of field research.

I have tried to keep the title as simple and straightforward as possible, but it may be informative to articulate and define more precisely what I mean.

Selecting: This is the simplest of the three words to understand; it refers to purposive or conscious choice in which selection is determined on the basis of explicitly stated procedures.

Ethnographic: This is a much more ambiguous term. Ethnography has been simultaneously viewed as a means and an end or both process and product (Agar, 1980; Van Maanen, 1988). The process of ethnography (e.g., participant observation) constitutes more of a strategy than a method (Bernard, 1988). As such, ethnography can and should include multiple approaches, including both qualitative and quantitative methods (Bernard, 1988; Fielding & Fielding, 1987; Pelto & Pelto, 1979), involving data that are both primary and secondary (documents). The ultimate aim or product of ethnography is a written account or representation of the total aspect of a society, culture, or social scene (Agar, 1980; Van Maanen, 1988).

Informants: For the sake of this volume, I will follow a convention that classifies those being studied as subjects, respondents, or informants. Although these three classifications can be envisioned as a continuation from the formal (subject) to the more informal (informants), there are certainly cases in which individuals can be any combination of the three, either simultaneously or sequentially. Thus, for example, an individual can be a respondent who eventually takes on the role of informant.

Subjects are generally associated with more formal or experimental contexts. In such cases a subject may be asked, most often under laboratory conditions, to perform a cognitive or perceptual task or react to a set or sets of stimuli. Respondents, on the other hand, are generally thought of as individuals who respond to more structured or formal surveys. Such respondents tend to be chosen on a random basis and interviewed in more naturalistic or nonlaboratory settings. Finally, informants are individuals who tend to be interviewed in a more semistructured or informal, in-depth, detailed manner in a naturalistic setting. Informants are often selected on the basis of their attributes, such as access to certain kinds of information or knowledge that itself may be a function of such things as social status, position in an organization, or comprehension of cultural knowledge. Also, individuals can move back and forth among the three roles. Subjects can become informants, as when an individual is chosen for more in-depth interviewing (becoming an informant) on the basis of his or her approach to an experimental task (as a subject). Additionally, a respondent can become an informant because of particular attributes identified in the course of a survey (e.g., occupation and social status).

Ultimately, in this volume I am interested in discussing, within the context of a multimethod ethnographic approach, the rationale and procedures for selecting ethnographic informants. In the pages that follow, that which is systematic in ethnography is examined. This is not to say that opportunism and serendipity do not play a role in the ethnographic process. One cannot deny that luck, opportunism, serendipity, chance, and fortune have played roles in even the most scientific of enterprises (Kirk & Miller, 1986), let alone the uncertain realm of ethnographic research. However, matters of luck are by definition things not planned for and, therefore, are difficult to explicate in a book such as this. Thus we must place luck and opportunism, clearly important aspects of discovery in science, in relation to explicitly stated theories and methods. It is to such methodological and epistemological issues that we now turn.

Ethnographic Quality Versus Quantity

In sociology, and to some extent in anthropology, the ethnographic strategy has been associated more with various qualitative methods than with quantitative ones. Although there have been methods books that have been sensitive to linking the two methods (e.g., Bernard, 1988; Fielding & Fielding, 1987; Pelto & Pelto, 1979; Van Maanen, 1983), it is nevertheless the case that fieldwork, participant observation, and ethnography are more freely associated with that which is qualitative. Thus ethnography has been variously described in terms of "thick description" (Geertz, 1973) and "an interpretive act" (Van Maanen, 1988).

A good example of this association and the resulting quantitative/qualitative debate are two articles appearing in a 1986 issue of the *American Behavioral Scientist*. One is titled "Ethnographic and Qualitative Research Design and Why It Doesn't Work" (Borman, LeCompt, & Goetz, 1986); the other is appropriately titled "What Quantitative Research Is and Why It Doesn't Work" (Krenz & Sax, 1986). Borman et al.'s (1986) criticism of qualitative methods, particularly ethnography, is that it is too subjective, too value laden, not replicable, not generalizable, trivial in its conclusions, lacking internal validity, not empirical, neither rigorous nor systematic (i.e., unscientific), and doesn't prove anything. Krenz and Sax (1986) countercharge that in quantitative research, there is little correspondence between measures and "reality" and that such research has produced little "truth" that is useful in the context of educational practice. They go on to criticize the sloppy use of statistics and the problems inherent in a lack of understanding of causality.

These charges and countercharges are indicative of the ongoing debate in the social sciences between the positivist and subjectivist camps (Pinxten, 1981). Fortunately, there are social science researchers who do not see the exclusivity of these approaches in the course of investigating a wide range of social science theories. There is a middle ground (Kirk & Miller, 1986; Miles & Huberman, 1984; Pinxter, 1981; Whyte, 1984).

In Search of Rules for Qualitative Research

According to Borman et al. (1986), "Qualitative research is criticized for having no hard-and-fast rules of procedure; design and method for data collection are not specified in advance, and variables do not appear to be either measurable or defined in operational terms" (p. 52). Such impressions of qualitative research, particularly within the discipline of anthropology, are understandable when one reviews the type of methodological training that has traditionally been imparted to students of ethnography — characterized by McCracken (1988) as "little if any."

Two stories help illustrate this tradition in anthropology. In the first chapter of *Research Methods in Cultural Anthropology*, Bernard (1988) relates a story told by Charles Wagley, who Bernard identifies as "one of the best ethnographers our discipline has ever produced" (p. 9). Wagley asked Alfred Kroeber, one of the founding fathers of anthropology, for some advice on teaching field methods. According to Wagley (1983), who was hoping for some constructive help, Kroeber replied, "Some can and some can't" (p. 1), with nothing more being said on the subject. After relating this, Wagley goes on to say that he taught the course on field methods anyway, but remembers little about its content or organization and never taught it again.

A similar story is conveyed in the first two pages of Agar's (1980) *The Professional Stranger*. According to Agar, the Berkeley graduate student folklore during the 1960s went something like this:

A graduate student at the end of her first year, was given a few hundred dollars by the department and told to go and study an Indian group during the summer. Not only had no one told her how to do ethnography; neither had anyone bothered to describe the location of the tribe.

With trembling heart and sweaty palms, she approached the door of Kroeber himself for some advice. After several passes by the open door, she entered and nervously cleared her throat. Kroeber was typing (naturally) and did not look for a minute or so. When he did, the student explained her dilemma and asked for advice. "Well," said Kroeber, returning to his typing, "I suggest you buy a notebook and a pencil." (p. 2)

Whether these tales are true or not, both stories make the point that there has been a general lack of explicit, identifiable, transferable procedures for conducting ethnographic research. This "trial by fire" approach added greatly to the mystique of fieldwork, but did little to aid the uninitiated or to increase skeptics' (e.g., granting agencies) understanding of the important qualities of the ethnographic approach (Miles & Huberman, 1984). A consequence of this persistence of the unstated and unwritten in the method of ethnography has been constant reinvention and a lack of accumulated strategic knowledge (Miles & Huberman, 1984).

Fortunately, this is changing in anthropology, as there are more books and articles exploring the ethnographic strategy that are revealing its strengths and weaknesses as well as describing its procedures. It is interesting to note that these recent discussions of ethnography span the entire spectrum of philosophical perspectives (e.g., compare Marcus, 1986, with Bernard, 1988).

Sociology, too, initially lacked any standardized or explicit ethnographic method (Kirk & Miller, 1986). As quoted in Kirk and Miller (1986), Anderson, perhaps sociology's first participant observer, reports that "the only instruction I recall from Park was, 'Write down only what you see, hear, and know, like a newspaper reporter'" (p. 40). Significantly more discussion of the status of ethnography and its method has taken place since (see Adler & Adler, 1987). In addition, the legacy of the Chicago school, which stressed a search for the "facts," in combination with the predominance of American urban field sites, forced sociologists to be concerned with a whole range of factors not faced by anthropologists, who generally studied the exotic (i.e., non-Western and nonliterate societies). Sociologists had to defend their findings against their natives, as well as against their academic peers. After all, most of the people sociologists study are literate and can read the ethnographic product. Furthermore, the peer community of sociologists (and other social scientists) is made up of members of the culture or society usually studied, and therefore are often self-proclaimed experts. This has led ethnographies in sociology to be less sweeping in their claims and has had the additional feature of forcing sociologists to be more forthright in describing the methods of ethnography, since such description is crucial in defending their findings.

Finally, I want to note that, for the most part, cultural anthropology has never experienced any appreciable quantitative movement in the discipline, but sociology has become predominantly quantitative. Sociologists who were practitioners of ethnography had to defend their chosen research strategy from the rest of sociology, which often viewed ethnography and qualitative methods as less than scientific, not reliable, possibly suffering from lack of internal or external validity, and not replicable. This is not to say that qualitative sociologists ran out and immediately embraced the dicta of science; this was certainly not the case. However, a real dialogue comparing and contrasting the two approaches forced sociologists to be considerably more aware of the need to articulate the methods of their research, or at least to debate the epistemological and philosophical advantages of each more vigorously than did anthropologists (Kirk & Miller, 1986). The forums for these debates were field settings, journals, professional meetings, symposia, and even departmental gatherings ("corridor politics"). Since cultural anthropology essentially escaped what McCracken (1988) calls "the winter of positivism that prevailed in the social sciences in the 1960s and 1970s" (p. 14), the anthropological practitioners of ethnography could be complacent, given they had to defend little from either nonliterate natives or their anthropological peers. In their book on qualitative approaches, Miles and Huberman (1984) also recognize the lack of articulation of qualitative methods:

> The methodological sections of most reports of qualitative studies are thin. Methodological articles on analysis issues and approaches are all too rare. We believe that anyone who wants to advance the craft of qualitative analysis owes it to colleagues to communicate what has been learned to others. We advise stronger methodological emphasis in articles and books drawn from qualitative data, and encourage reports of training methods in courses and workshops that have successfully expanded analysis skills. (p. 252)

I should digress here a moment and report that this is not to say that there has been no important methodological work on developments in anthropology. To the contrary, much of the early work in ethnoscience or the "new ethnography" and the more recent work in cognitive anthropology has certainly made important contributions to an explicit methodology (e.g.,

Boster, 1986; Boster & Johnson, 1989; D'Andrade, 1976; Garro, 1986; Metzger & Williams, 1966; Tyler, 1969). In addition, the earlier works of Pelto and Pelto (1979) and, more recently, Bernard (1988) show a definite awareness of the need for more explicit ethnographic strategies in anthropology.

An important element in making the method of ethnography less mysterious and more accessible to both practitioners and outsiders (e.g., funding agencies) is a more open and explicit discussion of how we, as ethnographers, come to know what we know. One small step toward this end is an increased awareness concerning the need to document more carefully, on both theoretical and methodological grounds, our procedures for the selection of informants. As Werner and Schoepfle (1987) point out, this has rarely been done:

> The selection of consultants for ethnographic fieldwork is often shrouded in mystery. Very few ethnographers list explicitly the number of people they have talked to. . . . Ethnographers are equally reluctant to explain how they selected the people they did talk to. Some of this reluctance is understandable, since ethnographic samples are usually opportunistic: Ethnographers interview whomever they are able to convince to cooperate. This sounds like a cop-out, and sometimes it is. (p. 183)

Lack of explicit discussion of the bases for informant selection impedes the comparability of ethnographic studies. It is to the idea of comparability that we now turn.

Replication and the Ethnographic Enterprise: The Sociology of Replication

An important aspect of science is *replication*, which simply refers to the independent verification of research results through repeated experimentation, observation, and so on (Brim & Spain, 1974). Although it is one of the main components of science, it is certainly not its most glamorous, nor does research in this mode generally lead to fame. It is probably the dullest part of science, but it is important nevertheless.

Probably the best recent example illustrating this point is the controversy concerning the discovery of cold fusion. The announcement that fusion can be produced at room temperature created quite a stir among members of the scientific community. The researchers claiming this incredible discovery were two chemists by the names of Stanley Pons and Martin Fleischmann.

Soon after their announcement, labs all over the world rushed to replicate the original experiment. One lab claimed replication, but another, and then yet another, could not seem to duplicate the results. Evidence began to accumulate that cast doubt on the claims of the two researchers (Waldrop, 1989).

Failure to replicate the original findings was partially blamed on the incomplete disclosure of experimental design by Pons and Fleischmann. Accusations of unethical and unscientific behavior began to emerge. Rumors spread to the effect that the chemists prematurely announced their findings in a public forum, instead of through the usual peer process (i.e., scientific journals), in order to obtain large amounts of grant money (Crawford, 1989). Whether cold fusion proves to be fact or fiction in the future, the importance of independent verification through replication cannot be denied in this case.[1]

Had cold fusion been repeatedly replicated by independent labs, Pons and Fleischmann would have been guaranteed to win the Nobel Prize. Science as we know it would have been revolutionized, textbooks would have to be rewritten, and the accumulated knowledge would lead us to possibly even greater discoveries. However, Pons and Fleischmann are famous, or should I say infamous, no matter what the reality, in contrast to the many individuals who enthusiastically attempted replication. These individuals and labs will generally remain nameless, particularly with respect to the public. Even though they provided an invaluable service to the cause of science, they will receive but little recognition, let alone something like a Nobel Prize. Replication is essential, but it is not what careers are made of (*In Search of the Double Helix* provides a good illustration of this).

Innovation—being on the cutting edge or being at the frontiers of the discipline—is to many scholars what is important, fulfilling, and maximally rewarding.[2] But some independent verification of research findings must take place if knowledge is to be accumulated and theory advanced (Romney, 1989). In the natural sciences, although often dull, replication is a common practice. In social science, it is rarely done. Why this is the case is far more complex than simple matters of glamour or career, although the following insight by Pelto and Pelto (1979) certainly indicates that these factors do play a role in understanding the lack of replication in anthropology:

A principal weakness in much anthropological work is that investigation is not recycled. Most frequently, the social scientist who has finished a neat piece of work publishes the conclusions and then moves on to another somewhat related area of research — to expand on the supposedly successful model of explanation — rather than submitting it to critical retesting. It is not difficult to see that there are important features in the general culture of the social sciences that encourage poor methodology. Pressures to publish — and to produce *new* and *novel* conceptualizations — encourage premature closure of investigation. And our social-science culture provides too few rewards for patient investigation, recycling, and replication of research. Instead of hearing applause for a replication of observations, the anthropologist more often hears a scornful "That's already been done by _____, ten years ago." (p. 286)

The debate in the social sciences as to whether replication is feasible or should even be of concern is an important one. Some of this stems from the view, for example, that qualitative studies are difficult to reproduce (Jick, 1983); even if one wanted to engage in replication, authors often give such limited information concerning methods and research design that it is virtually impossible to do so (Miles & Huberman, 1984). As reported in Pelto and Pelto (1979), Gloscock and Kimble studied 400 publications from anthropology journals in terms of their detailed reporting of methods and research design. Out of these 400 articles, only 3% provided sufficient information to enable replication of some kind. The ability to replicate is primarily a function of whether the researcher has provided clear operational definitions of the subject matters studied (Bernard, 1988), the specifications of research practices, or, generally, details on what was actually done (Lastrucci, 1963).

Ethnography, particularly in anthropology, is notorious for lack of replication. Aside from the lack of rewards for such endeavors, there are probably other factors at work. First, field research, unlike experiments or even survey research, is an extremely time-consuming process. Although experiments can often be replicated in just weeks, the replication of field research may involve, at the very least, one or two years. The thought that an ethnographer would invest large amounts of professional time in an endeavor (replication) that yields few professional rewards is quite unrealistic.[3]

Second, ethnographers' personal possessiveness of the fieldwork setting leads them to talk of "their" villages or "my" natives. This territoriality is often respected among ethnographers, so that there almost always exists an implicit norm or taboo against studying another ethnographer's village or Indians or questioning the validity of his or her findings (Kirk & Miller, 1986). Thus ethnographers jealously guard the identities of their informants or other sources of data, possibly feeling they are somehow protecting their natives, leading to the "laundering" of reports (Douglas, 1976). This may sound cynical, but such nondisclosure of various kinds of information impedes chances for the production of comparable work in other places.[4] I know such possessiveness exists, since it reared its ugly head during my first major bit of field research. In this case, there were a number of anthropologists working in "my" village. I tried to deny its existence, but possessiveness was there.

Third, and related to the second point, ethnographers have a huge personal investment in their ethnographic research. Such an investment may lead some to guard "trade" secrets. Thus explicit description of one's methods or procedures may open one up for the possibility of being accused of having used incorrect logic or just simply being wrong. Being wrong is one thing, but being wrong after such an investment of time and effort is quite another. If the Lewis-Redfield debates and the heated and vicious Mead-Freeman controversy are any indication of the usual outcomes of confirmatory activities, then it is no wonder verification, as it has traditionally been practiced, is such an unpopular enterprise among field researchers.

Fourth, the nonscientific histories of many of the social science disciplines that use ethnography have limited attention to issues of replication. This is particularly exemplified by the historical difference between sociology and anthropology and their concern for documentation of research methods (e.g., data collection procedures, whether "qualitative" or otherwise).

Finally, the ritualistic, dues-paying nature of field research has left it shrouded in mystery. Ethnographers are proud of their field experiences, often having survived horrendous conditions in the field. "War stories" are an important part of ethnographic talk (Kirk & Miller, 1986), and when several experienced field researchers get together, they eagerly exchange such stories; in fact, exchange of such stories may be a necessary prerequisite of being allowed into the conversation. The application of standard, reproducible methods in the field will potentially remove some of this mystique, and possibly make ethnography dull and predictable, more like survey or experimental research.

As Pelto and Pelto (1979) state, there has been some indication that increasingly open debates are taking place concerning the method of ethnography in anthropology: "Open discussion of ethnographers' experiences and methods is removing some of the mystique of field work and is helping to identify those aspects that can be made more explicitly operational" (p. 177). Increasing openness, in combination with more attention to multimethod approaches and triangulation, is improving the chances for replication in ethnographic research (Bernard, 1988; Fielding & Fielding, 1987; Jick, 1983; McClintock, Brannon, & Maynard-Moody, 1983; Pelto & Pelto, 1979). However, it is unrealistic to believe that replication, in the strictest sense, will ever be a part of the ethnographic enterprise.

But perhaps it is the replication of specific tests of hypotheses drawn from theory in different contexts that is ultimately the most valuable. The best that can be hoped for is what I term *partial replication*. In this form of replication, only portions of other studies are repeated or compared. This has the distinct advantage of maintaining the uniqueness and newness of research while providing critically important retests or independent verifications of portions of earlier research. Under such a scenario, a researcher can both contribute to the cutting edge and, at the same time, add to the accumulation of knowledge. This form of replication is much more common in, for example, research in social psychology, where a study may expand on earlier research by explaining its validity in different contexts or with the use of different controls (e.g., Freeman, Roeder, & Mulholland, 1979).[5] The research in this case has the potential to contribute new knowledge while confirming or disconfirming our current state of knowledge.

Examples of "secondary" applications of these ideas are the areas of meta-analysis (Glass, 1976; Rosenthal, 1984) and comparative analysis (Dow, 1989). In its simplest form, meta-analysis summarizes quantitatively studies involving measures of associations between related independent and dependent variables, coming up with a single aggregate measure of association to estimate the hypothesized effect. In comparative analysis, studies or cases (e.g., Human Relations Area File, a cross-cultural data base) are compared to explore or test hypotheses, concerning, for example, the association of traits across various societies. In either case, the validity of theoretical outcomes depends on the extent to which there were standard operational definitions or measures across all the studies. The validity of the final comparisons depends upon the comparability of the original studies. Such comparability can be achieved only through the use of standardized or well-specified methods, measures, and definitions.

Similarly, in a "primary" application, standardized or explicitly stated methods are also essential. This is particularly important for comparisons in ethnography. The emergent nature of field research makes it next to impossible ever to duplicate exactly the methods and experiences of another ethnographer.[6] Differences in personal and other skills between ethnographers lend to this difficulty. In addition, one cannot count on the same luck or serendipity experienced by an ethnographer whose study one is trying to repeat. Yet, in attempting to carry out partial replication, one is not trying to replicate the study in every detail — just certain aspects of it. Repeatability of such cases is enhanced if methods, theoretical assumptions, and operational definitions are explicitly stated.

I believe some of my own fieldwork in Alaska helps illustrate this point (Johnson, 1981; Miller & Johnson, 1981). The position I maintained at a fish camp (converted cannery) was contingent upon my skills as a boat carpenter and the fact that I happened, fortuitously, to find an opening for a carpenter in the camp, a highly paid and sought-after position. This position as an actual participant in the system gave me exceptional access to people and information (e.g., cannery records). It would be highly unlikely that another ethnographer could be in the right place, at the right time, and with the right skills. This is not to say that someone with boat carpentry skills could not find a position in a fish camp with some amount of effort. It could happen, but it is unlikely. However, there were portions or aspects of my field research that could be repeated irrespective of one's role as participant observer or complete participant.

In investigating the social organization of the fish camp, I applied a common standardized data collection task called a pile sort (Weller & Romney, 1988). As shall be shown in later chapters, this technique was useful for exploring the perceived basis for social organization in the fish camp. This technique is exportable and could easily be readministered in other fish camps and salmon canneries in the region. Thus perceived factors for organization of the fishermen (e.g., ethnicity, bunkhouse residence, aptitude as a fisherman) could easily be compared across studies.

Another means of verification is called staggered replication (Miles & Huberman, 1984; Stake & Easley, 1978). This form of replication takes place within or across sites. Thus researchers validate the findings in one site through testing in other sites. In addition, verification can be within a single study, as when earlier findings are tested or verified some time in a future phase of the same study.

Whether one believes in the independent verification of field research or not, it is clear that there should be, at the very least, concern for partial replication, staggered replication, or comparability of research findings if theory is to be advanced. In any event, explicitness of the research process, including research design and methods, will aid in eliminating discrepancies and can lead to the further accumulation of knowledge. The use of explicit and conscious procedures for the selection of ethnographic informants is just one small part of this need for greater specification. It is, nevertheless, an important part.

It should be noted that the selection of informants is an involved process that includes not only establishing conscious criteria for selection, but also issues surrounding establishing informant rapport, ethics in the field, protection of information sources under extreme circumstances (e.g., studies of the drug trade), and so on. These are all important concerns and should definitely be considered in designing ethnographic research. However, such matters are beyond the scope of this book. The reader should be aware of how these concerns may influence purposive choice and the subsequent disclosure of information concerning informants.

NOTES

1. The controversy still goes on, with recent claims of bursts of detectable neutrons lending support to the actual discovery of cold fusion (Hively, 1989).

2. Glaser and Strauss (1967) note that sociology is like physics in that the highest rewards go to those scientists who produce new theories. They support this by saying that six of the eight MacIver Awards up until 1967 had gone to sociologists for their contribution to grounded theory.

3. Being the first to study a village or neighborhood is analogous to anthropologist as explorer. Subsequent research in an area is less exciting and often difficult, depending on the behavior of previous ethnographers (e.g., the extent to which previous ethnographers have offended the villagers).

4. This is not to say that an ethnographer should not protect the identity of his or her informants. However, details as to the rationales for selection should be provided, as long as the anonymity of the informant can be maintained.

5. A journal dedicated to replication in social psychology was started in 1979. It lasted for only one or two volumes.

6. This is similar to Kirk and Miller's (1986) discussion of quixotic reliability. No researcher should be expected to have to use the same instrument and laboratory as the original researcher in replicating an experiment.

2. THE PROBLEMS
OF INFORMANT SELECTION

Discussions concerning the rationale for the selection of informants in field research are by no means new. Mead (1953) was particularly concerned about what has been termed by Honigmann (1970) anthropological sampling or nonprobability sampling. She stressed the importance of the selection of informants by their salient characteristics, so that the validity of information could be maximized. Other early researchers were also concerned with such matters. Spindler (1955), for example, chose informants on the basis of socioeconomic status and extent of cultural participation.

Mead (1953) believed anthropological sampling was an important and valid aspect of field research. She came to its defense, putting forth discussions of bias and other possible violations to the validity of this approach. Much of this defense was in reaction to the requirements of probability sampling, in which bias and sample size are critical in determining confidence in the research findings:

> The validity of the sample depends not so much upon the number of cases as upon the proper specification of the informant, so that he or she can be accurately placed, in terms of a very large number of variables — age, sex, order of birth, family background, life-experience, temperamental tendencies (such as optimism, habit of exaggeration, etc.), political and religious position, exact situational relationship to the investigator, configurational relationship to every other informant, and so forth. Within this extensive degree of specification, each informant is studied as a perfect example, an organic representation of his complete cultural experience. (p. 646)

The contrast between probability and nonprobability sampling rests to a great extent on the idea of bias. Probability sampling in its simplest form assumes equal probability of observation of all sampling units in the universe studied. A random sample smaller than the population as a whole should yield a representative picture of that population. The larger the sample, the more confidence one has in the precision of the picture. Thus a true random sample of a population should, for example, yield proportions of units (e.g., the ratio of Blacks to Whites in a population) that approximate what would be found in the population. Sample statistics are maximum likelihood estimates of population parameters.

In reality, however, a true random sample is not always possible, particularly in field research, since it is often difficult to know the universe a priori or to have what is called a "sampling frame" (Bernard, 1988). In addition, in large populations, small random samples may not capture sufficient numbers of cases that are of theoretical interest. Thus if a researcher is interested in an ethnic group that represents only a small percentage of the total population, a straight random sample of the population may not yield enough cases from this ethnic group to make a study possible. For these reasons, researchers often use cluster or stratified sampling in order to ensure an adequate number of cases for the theoretical investigation at hand. This is also similar to Cook and Campbell's (1979) "model of deliberate sampling for heterogeneity." Bernard (1988) and Pelto and Pelto (1979) provide more detailed discussions of these sampling procedures and probability samples more generally.

The bases on which samples of this kind are stratified or clustered are determined on theoretical grounds. Thus if, for example, the independent variable "ethnicity" has some hypothesized effect on the dependent variable "unemployment," then the theoretical notion that ethnicity is important in this context influences the construction of strata for the sample. If the researcher's assumption that ethnicity affects unemployment is not correct, then sample strata based on ethnicity may introduce unknown error of some kind (Bernard, 1988).

The concerns of Mead (1953) and others (Honigmann, 1970; Spindler, 1955) about proper specifications that ensure the representativeness of their nonprobability samples or choice of informants are similar to the specifications or assumptions surrounding the determination of clusters or strata in a stratified probability sample. If the logic on which each was selected is valid, so too will be the sample. Thus, in both cases, factors deemed theoretically important determine the criteria for selection.

This is not to say that probability and nonprobability selection procedures produce the same thing. As noted, probability sampling, under optimal conditions, yields the researcher a representative picture of various features of the population. Given valid theoretical assumptions, nonprobability samples yield a small number of informants who provide representative pictures of aspects of information or knowledge distributed within the population. Whereas in stratified samples one is attempting to minimize within-strata variance and maximize between-strata variance in the selection of respondents, among informants one is attempting to minimize variation in knowledge or information for a single informant or cluster of related informants while maximizing variation in knowledge among other individual informants or clusters in which knowledge or information is homogeneous. Thus one may wish to select informants from groups that are maximally homogeneous and comparably heterogeneous across informants or informant clusters, as in differences between the knowledge of experts and novices (Boster & Johnson, 1989) or between curers and noncurers (Garro, 1986). Tremblay (1957) points out some of these very factors in his discussion of the selection of key informants:

In using key informants, one chooses them strategically, considering the structure of the society and the content of the inquiry. Furthermore, in the interview itself, although the informant is given latitude to choose his own order and manner of presentation, there is a systematic attempt on the part of the researcher to cover completely the topic under analysis. When we use key informants, we are not randomly sampling from the universe of characteristics under study. Rather, we are selectively sampling specialized knowledge of the characteristics. (p. 689)

Glaser and Strauss's (1967) discussion of theoretical sampling is a good example of the notion of comparability across a range of diverse groups and its usefulness in the generation of grounded theory. They also note the importance of minimizing and maximizing differences among groups in order to discover categories and help identify emergent theoretical properties.

Arnold (1970) suggests what he calls "dimensional sampling" for studies using only a small number of cases. The goal of this approach "is to provide a framework for drawing a purposive sample representative of the universe to which one wishes to generalize" (p. 147). In this framework, one would clearly lay out the dimensions on which cases vary. Representative cases are then taken from each of the contrastive features of the dimension, thus protecting against bias. In another example, Seidler (1974) recommends using what he calls "instrumental" theory to guide the selection of informants. By doing so, the researcher will be better able to "pinpoint sources of bias and error in measurement" (p. 825). It is important to note the differences between the approaches of Arnold and Seidler, on the one hand, and of Glaser and Strauss, on the other. Whereas the former stress the use of prior theoretical knowledge in constructing a framework, the latter stress the importance of the emergent nature of the within-group and between-group comparisons, eventually leading to the discovery of categories that can help in developing grounded theory. I refer to the first as a *theory-driven* framework and to the latter as a *data-driven* or exploratory framework.

Werner and Schoepfle (1987) are also concerned about sampling informants within a social system. They view ethnographic sampling as the complementary use of both ethnographic and survey techniques. Using an archaeological metaphor, they liken ethnographic sampling to surface surveys and the digging of test trenches. The former provide superficial, wide coverage of an area, while in the latter digging is focused in areas where finds are anticipated. In this view, such procedures as random sampling,

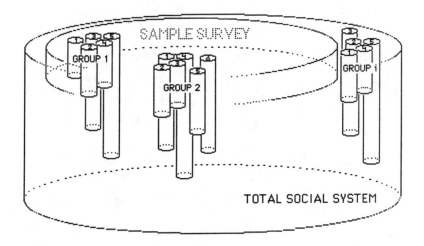

Figure 2.1   Survey and Ethnographies: Covering a Social System Composed of
              Small Group Cultures

SOURCE: Werner and Schoepfle (1987).

stratified random sampling, systematic sampling, and cluster sampling in which one uses a questionnaire are analogous to a surface survey. The analogy to the test trenches would be a small group ethnography.

A series of figures used by Werner and Schoepfle (1987) illustrates both the relationship between survey and ethnographic techniques and the coverage through a system each provides. Figures 2.1 and 2.2 show coverage of a social system in which both small group cultures and informants (consultants) are the focus. Identification of groups can come, for example, from a "baseline ethnography" involving a network sample of groups. Identification of consultants is based on a baseline ethnography involving a cross-sectional approach. Werner and Schoepfle go on to describe these two approaches this way:

> The cross-sectional approach is the most common compromise between ethnography as the naturalistic study of small group cultures and an ethnography of a larger social unit, such as a tribe. Each consultant is a member of some social group, and in the ideal case, also an expert on some aspect of daily life.

> In each of the cases mentioned here, the ethnographer faces a different problem for selecting a sample for ethnographic study. In the first case, the

26

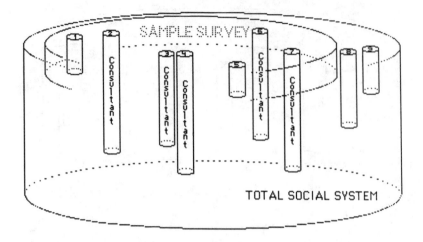

Figure 2.2   Cross-Sectional Ethnography and Survey
SOURCE: Werner and Schoepfle (1987).

selection of the right small groups for intensive study is crucial. Ethnographers may be aided in this selection by previous knowledge of the social system. Alternatively, they must focus early intensive efforts on identifying the key groups in the social system.

The sampling in the cross-sectional ethnography is a little easier. Ethnographers need not have an intimate knowledge of the social organization that exists within the social system. Instead, they can start with an opportunistic sample, or a "networking" sample. These contacts may soon lead to the right specialists, especially if the initial ethnographic efforts concentrate on identifying the people with the desired specialties. (p. 189)

Miles and Huberman (1984) suggest three solutions for the reduction of bias relevant to informant selection. First, they recommend simply increasing the number of cases. Although this seems to make sense on the surface, particularly in light of statistical wisdom, one should proceed with caution. As we shall see, a small number of specially chosen informants can yield more valid and generalizable information than a larger group of general informants (Campbell, 1955). Simply increasing the number without increasing strategic coverage of the system may only increase the chances for bias. Second, Miles and Huberman recommend taking into account more contrasting cases. This will increase the chances of gaining a broader perspective and will aid in identifying potential bias due to informants' stakes in specific outcomes or their positions in an organization (Seidler, 1974). This supports other research suggesting that marginal natives who are solid insiders (Agar, 1980) or cynical natives (Bernard, 1988) make good informants because of their particular perspectives. Finally, the systematic, theoretically determined sorting of cases will ensure more complete coverage of the phenomena under study.

These last two recommendations are particularly important. As Miles and Huberman (1984) note, these correspond to ideas surrounding stratification and randomization in survey research, precisely some of the ideas discussed in an earlier portion of this chapter. Moreover, the final recommendation is crucial in that it suggests the importance of a structured, theoretical rationale for the selection of cases as manifested in such things as substructures or typologies. Such devices can provide for the selection of representative cases, given that the underlying theory used to construct them is valid.

In light of the discussion, I see two types of representativeness. The first is simply that which is statistically representative. We know it is representative because sampling theory tells us so, given we did things right (i.e., big enough and random). It should be noted that informants can be selected on the basis of statistical representativeness, as when the selection of ethnographic informants is based on inherent variations in the structure of survey data. Selected cases from a survey can be used for an in-depth study of features of the sample data, as when cases are selected for being the most or least acculturated in a factor analysis (Robbins, Williams, Kilbride, & Pollnac, 1969). This will be examined in more depth in Chapter 4.

The second is theoretical representativeness. Under these circumstances, the ethnographer chooses informants from segments of a social system that are meaningful in terms of the ethnographer's explicitly stated theories, hypotheses, or hunches (e.g., substructures, typologies, categories, network subgroups) as to the workings of the society, culture, or phenomenon under study. As long as these theoretical assumptions are valid, so too will be the ethnographic sample of informants.

Criteria for Selection

Much of the kind of nonprobability sampling discussed so far refers to what is called "purposive" (Warwick & Lininger, 1975), "strategic" (Hunt,

1970), or "judgment" sampling (Bernard, 1988; Honigmann, 1970; Pelto & Pelto, 1979). Informants chosen for a specific reason or purpose are those informants selected on the basis of judgment sampling. As we have seen, selection is not ad hoc or opportunistic; rather, it is guided by an ethnographer's theoretically and experientially informed judgments. A good discussion of this is provided by Honigmann (1970):

> I am stressing the deliberateness with which any subjects are chosen. Informants selected by virtue of their status (age, sex, occupation) or previous experience, qualities which endow them with special knowledge that the ethnographer values, are chosen by a type of nonprobability sampling best called judgment sampling. The ethnographer uses his prior knowledge of the universe to draw representatives from it who possess distinctive qualifications. He may, for example, select informants or subjects according to class strata, occupational status, sex, age, or length of residence in the community. (p. 268)

Aside from the early work of Mead (1953) and others (Spindler, 1955; Tremblay, 1957), early discussions of informant choice were mostly superficial and involved little discussion of reliability, validity, or the specification of choice based on theoretical grounds. Probably the most classic discussion of informant selection in this mode is found in *Notes and Queries on Anthropology* (1951). The section on informant choice begins like this:

> The selection of informants will to some extent be determined by circumstances beyond the investigator's control. Certain hints on the choice of informants may, however, be useful.

> It may be well to explain what is meant by an informant. It is not suggested that these are necessarily individuals who come to the anthropologist and give information daily in answer to questions; every member of the society is a potential informant, his behaviour may be observed and his remarks noted. It is, however, extremely useful to train two or three intelligent people so that they understand the method of investigation and are able to act consciously as intermediaries and to give information with precision. Such informants can be especially useful to cultivate close acquaintance with a limited number of men and women of position, through whose agency it will be possible to start inquiries into such subjects as family life, crafts, religion and magic, etc. They may take the inquirer first to their homesteads, show their own crafts, and introduce him to their relatives and friends. They can act as guides and informants on special occasions and during ceremonies. (p. 43)

This discussion goes on to inform the ethnographer of the proper way to treat informants and the proper means for remuneration. Although much of this is superficial, one paragraph does briefly touch upon some of the issues discussed in this chapter. The following passage describes the importance of a potential informant's status and role on the kind of information one could hope to collect:

> Whenever possible, information should be obtained directly from specialists (priests, rain-makers, doctors, iron-workers, makers of special objects, etc.), and these should be visited and suitable presents made to them. They may be flattered by the attention, and willing to give regular information afterwards, but when very esoteric matters are concerned, they may have to be approached with great patience and diplomacy. It is unwise for an investigator to ask a specialist (especially one with religious or magical power) to visit him until a friendly relationship has been established. It is necessary also to obtain the opinion of ordinary people about specialists — their rules, qualifications, character, etc., in order to discover what such specialists mean to the lay community. (p. 44)

Although this passage alludes to the importance of attributes of informants in the acquisition of data, it provides little ground for understanding why informants should be selected on the basis of simply being specialists. Informant selection, like sampling rationale, cannot be truly discussed outside of any theory.

An early article by Tremblay (1957) discusses criteria for the selection of key informants for use in early phases of a large study. Wanting definitional, objective, and judgmental types of data from key informants, Tremblay sought information that could be used in the development of a survey instrument and in the preliminary selection of communities for study. First, he wanted to know what terms informants used to define and describe both poverty and wealth and to identify communities on the basis of these definitions as to each community's richness or poorness. Second, informants could help in defining the true boundaries of a community, in lieu of mostly inadequate formal boundaries such as school, postal, or electoral districts. Finally, key informants could add insights that could not otherwise be anticipated in the original research design.

To meet these objectives, Tremblay outlined five criteria on which to base the selection of the "ideal" informant. The first of these was "role in the community." By this, he meant the formal position an informant holds that would expose him or her to pertinent information. A second, and related, criterion was the knowledge informants possessed as a result of their respective role. The remaining three criteria were less a function of formal roles or associated knowledge and more a matter of the innate abilities of informants, including such things as willingness to communicate or cooperate, communicating ability, and impartiality. Tremblay recognized that the first criterion was the only one that could be determined a priori, while the remaining criteria served to cull informants:

> Of these five criteria of eligibility, only role in community can be determined in advance. The other qualifications are apt to be largely matters of personality, rather than positions in the social structure. Once individuals performing key roles in the economic structure are detected, the other four criteria serve as a screening device for separating the "good" from the "poorer" informants. This means that, after having prepared an ideal list of informants on the basis of their roles in the community, we could expect to make some changes as a result of personal contact and appraisal. It was also anticipated that repeated contacts with informants might lead to the best ones being singled out for more attention. (pp. 692-693)

Other ethnographers have noted similar criteria for the selection of informants. Bernard (1988) suggests choosing key informants on the more traditional grounds of "luck, intuition, and hard work by both parties to achieve a working relationship based on trust," as well as finding ones that are trustworthy, observant, reflective, articulate, and good storytellers (pp. 177-178). Spradley and McCurdy (1972) view a good informant as one who knows the culture well, is willing to talk, and is nonanalytical in communicating about his or her world. In the choice of consultants, a designation similar to key informants, Werner and Schoepfle (1987) see articulateness and thoughtfulness as two important criteria.

Choices made on the basis of formal role, position, or status may not always yield the best informants or the most informative ones. In their classic research on community leadership and decision making, Freeman, Fararo, Bloomberg, and Sunshine (1963) found three categories of leaders that have differential effects on community decision making. Leadership based on "social activity" was determined by the number of individual memberships in mostly voluntary organizations. Leadership based on "reputation" was a function of the top 41 most nominated as influential in a large survey's rankings of the most influential leaders in the community. Finally, "position" was based on the titular leaders in each of seven institutional areas. Freeman et al. found that those leaders identified by social activity overlapped little with those identified through either the positional or the reputational method. This has implications for the selection of informants in that reliance on formal positions alone in the ethnographic study of community decision making could yield a biased perspective. Potential informants should be considered on the basis of formal and informal roles, positions, and statuses. Many of the same ideas are found in the research on elites most exemplified by Domhoff (1970).

It is often the case that informal networks are the only means available for identifying and selecting informants. Kimball and Partridge (1979) found the concept of a social network invaluable in the study of cannabis use in a Colombian community. As Partridge moved from the formal to the more informal, the subject of study began to reveal itself; Kimball comments:

> But all such contacts were important to his objective of investigating cannabis in the life of the community; for, in following out the networks of social relationships, information was gained about the nature of the community and positions occupied by actors in the social organization of community life. (Kimball & Partridge, 1979, p. 60)

Partridge built upon and expanded these informal networks over the course of his fieldwork, which helped him to understand the nature of cannabis use in this community.

This use of informal networks in the selection of informants is discussed more explicitly by Werner and Schoepfle (1987). Claiming that most ethnographic sampling is opportunistic, haphazard, or less than explicit, they suggest building upon or expanding opportunistic samples through the use of social networks:

> After choosing anyone who cooperates, the next step is to follow a network. At first, one interviews those people who are easily accessible. Then, ethnographers use the help of this first batch of people to introduce them to a widening circle of friends and relations. The "networking" label derives from the fact that ethnographers utilize the personal networks of their earliest contacts to expand the sample. (pp. 183-184)

Based on an understanding of these social networks, the "well-informed informant" should emerge. Werner and Schoepfle view this as a way of identifying topical experts that has sound theoretical justifications.

Although Whyte (1984) might deny that a network paradigm is useful in selecting and understanding the value of informants, networks did play an undeniable role in his field research as reported in *Street Corner Society* (1955). Whyte's serendipitous introduction to Doc, an important "gate-keeper" among the people he wished to study, certainly had important structural implications for Whyte's research:

> Doc was an extraordinarily valuable informant. Whenever checked, his accounts seemed highly reliable. He was also well-informed about what was happening in his own and other groups and organizations in his district. This was due to the position he occupied in the community social structure. Other leaders discussed with him what they were doing and what they should do. Hence we knew developments in the "foreign relations" of the group before his followers, and usually in more direct and accurate form.

> Because of the wide variation in quality of informants, the researcher is always on the lookout for informants such as Doc, who can give a reasonably accurate and perceptive account of events. These special informants are frequently found at key positions in the communication structure, often as formal or informal leaders in the organization. They can weigh and balance the evidence themselves and correct for the distortions incorporated by their sources of information. Of course, they may withhold or distort information too, so wherever the researcher has to rely on secondhand reports he or she must be particularly cautious in his or her interpretation. (p. 127)

Similarly, Jacobs's (1977) study of an Illinois penitentiary demonstrates the importance of key positions in a network in that access to inmates, particularly gang members, was facilitated through the development of collaborative relations with gang leaders. Whyte (1984) cautions us to be careful about selecting informants simply on the basis of personality, and goes on to point out the importance of social structure in the selection of informants:

> It is not enough to assess the reliability of an informant simply in terms of the personality and character of the individual. We need also to recognize how the individual's position in the social structure is likely to shape his or her perceptions, recollections, and descriptions. (p. 127)

It is also true that social structure influences the distribution of knowledge through a system. Knowledge has consistently been mentioned as an important determinant in informant selection. In earlier anthropological work, particularly in linguistics and ethnoscience, it was assumed that one informant, or a few at the most, was all that was needed to illicit generalizable, valid, and reliable linguistic or cultural knowledge. After all, one aspect of culture is that it is shared, and intense interviews with one or a few of a culture's members should be sufficient. Some questioned these assumptions (Gardner, 1976; Manning & Fabrega, 1976) while yet others began to explore the very notion of intracultural variation (Berlin, Breedlove, & Raven, 1968; Fabrega & Manning, 1972; Pelto & Pelto, 1975; Pollnac, 1975). More recently, attempts have been made to understand variation in terms of the attributes of informants and their place in the intellectual division of labor (Boster 1985, 1986; Boster & Johnson, 1989; Boster, Johnson, & Weller, 1987; Garro, 1986; Kempton, 1981). This includes work on how cultural knowledge varies on the basis of exchange networks, kinship networks, residence (Boster, 1986), and position within an organization (Boster et al., 1987).

Variation in cultural knowledge has important implications for the selection of informants. The view that shared knowledge among individuals is a result of knowledge as to what is culturally "true" forms the basis for the cultural consensus model (Romney, Weller, & Batchelder, 1986). In this model, culture itself is viewed in terms of a consensus structure that allows for estimation of cultural knowledge and the determination of cultural competence of individuals (i.e., an individual's fit to the consensus). Thus some informants will be more culturally competent than others, and this relative competence can be considered in selecting knowledgeable informants. This model will be reviewed more fully, and an example provided, in Chapter 5.

What Can an Informant Tell Us?

When we seek out informants, we hope they will provide us with accurate and reliable information. I am not referring only to an informant's conscious effort to misinform or hold back information. Rather, the question is more a matter of what kinds of information we can realistically expect informants to know, recall, and report on accurately. In addition, how do social position, status, role, and all similar selective criteria affect the nature or accuracy of the information we seek?

In two classic and often-cited studies, Young and Young (1961) investigated interinformant reliability on agreement of information on a number of subjects, while Poggie (1972) compared key informants' responses to the findings of survey data. Young and Young found that interinformant agreement was high with regard to nonevaluative questions (e.g., Is there a church here?) but low for evaluative questions (e.g., How friendly are people here?). Poggie compared the responses of key informants who were mostly community leaders to the findings of a survey conducted in poorer communities. Each key informant was asked questions concerning life in his or her own community, and the answers were compared to the survey data. Poggie found that key informants' responses to questions pertaining to items that were more visible or observable (e.g., percentage of homes made of adobe) had a higher correspondence to the survey data than did their responses pertaining to less observable features of the community (e.g., percentage of people who eat bread daily).

Campbell (1955) provides an interesting study of the correlation between informants' rankings and rankings based on a survey on morale among submarine crews on ten ships. Campbell sought expert informants who had access to information concerning all ten ships. Since morale was considered to be a concern mostly of enlisted personnel (90% of the crews), it was felt that the best informants would come from the enlisted ranks, particularly from enlisted personnel at the squadron headquarters. In addition, Campbell felt that ideal informants should be "observant of the symptoms of morale" and "be willing and able to talk of them' " (p. 340).[1] Based on this rationale, yeoman-rated enlisted personnel performing office duties at the headquarters were selected as ideal informants. For comparison, the rankings of several officers from squadron headquarters were also obtained. These officers were of varying rank, were not in direct lines of command, and had no administrative duties requiring evaluation of ships or personnel. Informants' explanations of morale rankings, including specific incidents, were also collected.

Rankings by informants were compared to those obtained through survey techniques. Based on a "morale ballot" consisting of 30 questions concerning "potential complaints" and "expressions of dissatisfaction," a morale score for each ship was determined and the ship subsequently rank ordered on the basis of these scores. Spearman's rank-order correlation was used for comparison. The correlation between enlisted informants and the morale ballot was 0.9, while the correlation between officers and the morale ballot was 0.7 (combined, 0.8). All correlations are moderate to strong and statistically significant.

Two important factors are demonstrated by this study. First, in terms of certain kinds of quantitative information, key or expert informants can provide responses that are both valid and generalizable. Second, the differences in the magnitude of correlations involving the enlisted men (0.9), officers (0.7), and combined sample (0.8) suggest that a small number of specially selected informants are often better than a larger, extensive sampling of informants. As Campbell (1955) notes: "In this instance, at least, such exhaustive sampling of opinion proves inferior to the careful selection of a few informants" (p. 342). Thus those in the specialized group of enlisted personnel were the best informants for the problem at hand (i.e., they were better than the large combined group of informants). The moral to this story is that in the selection of informants, unlike in statistical sampling, bigger isn't always better!

There has been a recent controversy concerning the accuracy of informants in terms of their reports of behavior. A series of studies has questioned the long-standing tradition of relying on informants' reports of their network interactions (Bernard & Killworth, 1977; Bernard, Killworth, & Sailer, 1980, 1982; Killworth & Bernard, 1976, 1979). These studies eventually led the authors to scrutinize more closely the validity of retrospective data in general (Bernard, Killworth, Sailer, & Kronenfeld 1984).

The controversy led to an impressive flurry of research activity, including the reanalysis of the Bernard et al. (1980, 1982) data by independent researchers and the collection of new data to test propositions concerning informant accuracy. In such a reanalysis, Romney and Faust (1983) found that the accuracy of informants was related to the extent to which they interacted with others in the network; those who were more active were also the most accurate in reporting behaviors ($r = 0.52$). In a broader study of all four of Bernard et al.'s original data sets, Romney and Weller (1984) found that informant accuracy was highly correlated with informant reliability or each informant's correspondence to the aggregate ($0.79 \leq r \leq 0.98$). In a series of original studies tackling this same problem, it was found that informants are able to report more accurately on behavior that reflects regular and usual patterns (Freeman & Romney, 1987; Freeman, Romney, & Freeman, 1987). These are important studies because they show that many "validation" studies have overlooked the fact that their comparative standard — behavioral observations and measures — may also contain error. Moreover, the final two studies inform us that if we are interested in documenting regular, typical, and usual patterns of behavior, then we can have confidence in the verbal reports of our informants. That is, although

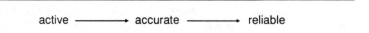

active ——————→ accurate ——————→ reliable

Figure 2.3   Relationship Between Activity in a Network and Accuracy and
Reliability

informants may have difficulty in reporting what they did last Tuesday, they can report accurately on usual patterns of behavior. In another study, Johnson and Miller (1986) found that the correspondence between behavior and cognition depends on the generalizability of the cognitive measure used. In this case, an unconstrained sorting task correlated higher with two behavioral measures than either behavioral measure correlated with the other.

These studies and their subsequent findings have important implications for the selection of informants in terms of reliability and the kinds of information we can expect informants to report on accurately. First, those informants who are most active in the network are those who are also more accurate and reliable in their reporting of behavior (see Figure 2.3). Thus this finding tends to support, in part, the conventional wisdom that "key" or central people make good informants (as Whyte discovered). Second, we can expect informants to be more reliable in their reporting of events that are usual, frequent, or patterned. Caution is warranted in asking informants to report accurately on the idiosyncratic or infrequent. In addition, this indicates that informants are good synthesizers of patterned information and that general questions or tasks will tap such knowledge (see Figure 2.4).

The Use of Stimulus Materials and Projective Aids

The reader will notice the extensive use of stimulus materials or projective aids (Whyte, 1984) in some of the examples in later chapters. Weller and Romney (1988) discuss the use of such techniques in an earlier volume in this series. These techniques have been used extensively in cognitive anthropology and have a long history in psychology. Collier (1957), for example, took pictures of houses in a community, along with some distinct

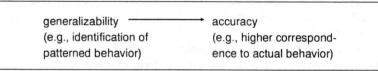

generalizability   ——————————→   accuracy
(e.g., identification of   (e.g., higher correspond-
patterned behavior)   ence to actual behavior)

Figure 2.4   Relationship Between Information Sought and Accuracy

work areas in a local factory. Informants' discussions of the pictures provided rich ethnographic detail. In addition, pictures of work areas facilitated interviews concerning work-related matters that were conducted in informants' homes.

Whyte (1984) discusses the use of a ranking procedure that involved informants' arrangements of cards in order of preference. The cards consisted of pieces produced by a team of workers at a glass works. Gaffers or servitors were asked to perform the task and explain their ranking behavior. Although no formal analysis of the rankings themselves was conducted, informants' explanations "revealed feelings about the work process that were not expressed in the ordinary interview" (Whyte, 1984, p. 108). Whyte goes on to say:

> We found the card-ranking method exceedingly useful in some cases in bringing out data on personality, status, and human relations. For example, one ambitious young gaffer evaluated his pieces primarily in terms of the degree of difficulty each design offered. The more complex the production problem, the more prestige to him if he succeeded. (p. 108)

Projective devices or stimulus materials can be useful in that they give informants the opportunity to pull together and discuss relationships among items, sometimes leading them to offer observations that, in a more direct interview approach, may be difficult to elicit. Use of these materials allows informants to focus on and visualize many concepts or items at a single moment, allowing for a discussion of more complex interrelationships and dimensions. That is to say, it allows informants the opportunity to express themselves in a systematic fashion (Boster & Johnson, 1989). In addition, the techniques can lead to inductive analysis of aggregated stimulus data (e.g., multidimensional scaling, factor analysis, correspondence analysis) that can lead to the generation of important theoretical dimensions of contrast — those dimensions that can aid in the selection of informants.

Summary

Criteria for selection of informants discussed so far are of two basic types. I will refer to the first of these two types, criteria concerning theoretical qualifications, as *criteria 1*. The second kind of criteria concern innate abilities; these will be termed *criteria 2*. These distinctions are similar to Tremblay's insightful discussion of those criteria known in advance (e.g., social role) versus those used as a "screening device" (e.g., informant cooperativeness). I use the term *theoretical qualifications* to emphasize the importance of theory in guiding the selection of informants in terms of such things as status, role, position, expertise, category or subgroup membership, dimensions, and even knowledge. Whereas these criteria are consciously specified, carefully researched, theoretically representative, and meaningful, the criteria concerning innate abilities become more a matter of personality, personal chemistry, interpersonal compatibility, the ability to establish a trusting relationship, and so on. The range of theoretically significant and representative informants is identified by the first set of criteria, while final choices may hinge on the second.

Procedures for determining what is theoretically representative in the sampling of informants falls within two basic frameworks. In some cases, the categories, positions, roles, and so on from which informants were selected were determined on the basis of a priori theoretical knowledge. In other cases, these categories or dimensions were emergent, being determined only sometime after the beginning of the study. Figure 2.5 illustrates these two fundamental means for determining representativeness. These frameworks are based on what is theory driven and what is data driven, as discussed earlier.

In the theory-driven case, criteria 1 factors are determined in advance on the basis of theoretical categories, classifications, dimensions, typologies, substructures, and so on (e.g., Arnold, 1970). Thus criteria 1 considerations may be determined on the basis of functional units within organizations, functional units that are known, a priori, to be of theoretical importance. On the other hand, in the data-driven or exploratory case, criteria 1 factors are determined on the basis of the discovery of emergent categories or dimensions (e.g., Glaser & Strauss, 1967). Thus representative informants can be chosen on the basis of their position along a single dimension, as in a factor analysis, or on the basis of informal subgroup membership. In either case, the same criteria 2 considerations of articulateness, personality, compatibility, and so on would influence final selection.

One final note about the difference between informants and key informants. To this point I have not made much of a distinction between the two. I have done this for a reason. It is essential to select key informants — individuals with whom ethnographers tend to work closely — from the pool of theoretically representative informants. By doing so, the ethnographer will have a more complete understanding of the potential biases associated with reliance on one or only a few informants. In addition, selecting from a pool of informants allows for increased chances of finding key informants who

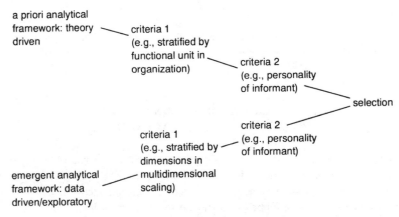

Figure 2.5   Selection of Informants Based on Criteria and Analytical Framework.

excel in terms of criteria 2 considerations or with whom an ethnographer can establish close personal relationships.

Finally, this having all been said, I can now describe the importance of informants not chosen on *conscious* grounds, but rather ones who are *fortuitously* uncovered. A great deal of ethnographic research has involved the use of informants serendipitously or opportunistically encountered, often involving the most unsystematic of choices. Such choices can be important in early research in the ethnographic enterprise, and the knowledge gained from these informants is not necessarily invalid. However, an ethnographer should retrospectively determine the theoretical representativeness of such informants in order to gain a more systemwide perspective recognizing any potential for bias. As long as there is an understanding of where such informants lie with respect to criteria 1 considerations, the ethnographer can place data obtained from opportunistically encountered informants within a theoretical framework.

The following three chapters will provide examples of informant selection in a variety of different contexts. Selection will be discussed in light of the analytical frameworks presented above and will move from theory-driven to more data-driven examples.

NOTE

1. Because of the requirement of ability to talk about morale, mechanically oriented specialists were not considered for selection, since the researcher felt that many had difficulty talking about social psychological intangibles.

3. SELECTION BASED ON AN A PRIORI FRAMEWORK

This chapter presents several examples that reflect the use of theory-driven frameworks in the selection of informants. The examples move progressively from more rigid applications of a priori knowledge to cases in which features of both frameworks are considered in the selection process.

The advantages of a multimethod ethnographic approach are evident in the examples in this chapter. On the one hand, qualitative data can be useful in the construction of survey instruments, sample designs, and hypotheses (Tremblay, 1957). On the other hand, survey results can help identify phenomena that require more in-depth qualitative investigation. Thus, aside from a demonstration of the use of a priori assumptions in determining choice criteria, this chapter also shows the mutually beneficial relationship between survey research and the selection of ethnographic informants.

Making Frameworks Concrete

To many, field research conjures up images of the intrepid ethnographer dressed in boots and khaki shorts, living among an isolated group of hunters and gatherers somewhere in the dense jungles of the Amazon. For others, ethnography may be best represented by the researcher who "hangs out" in the rough urban ghettos, trying to collect data from gang members, criminals, and their victims. However, field methods are as applicable in the boardrooms of corporate America as they are in the jungles of the Amazon or the streets of the ghetto. Although suitable for research in any setting, field research in organizations has some unique features. The application of an a priori framework is readily seen in a more bounded research setting, such as a formal organization.

Scott (1965) has observed that organizations are different from other collectives in terms of their members' being together in a common network of relations, sharing common values, and participating in a world that has a high degree of differentiation. In addition, organizations are formal, tend to be spatially and temporally fixed, have more specific and explicit objectives, and more formal restrictions on behavior. These all have implications for research design in terms of styles of participant observation, entry into the organization, and, ultimately, the selection of informants.

Given these particular features, an informant's representativeness, access to information, and knowledge will all be influenced by both formal and informal systems of differentiation. Dalton (1964), for example, sought not only informants — or intimates, as he called them — who could be trusted and counted on and who were open, nonprying, and not afraid to take risks, but also ones who had access to details concerning issues of interest. Dalton saw the number of informants as of less importance than other strategic factors: "Number seemed to me less important than the individual's position, reliability, and knowledge and the rapport achieved with him" (p. 66). Thus Dalton was concerned with both criteria 1 and criteria 2 considerations.

Unlike when conducting ethnographic research in other settings, formal roles and functional units and divisions in organizations are known in advance, and their features can be explicitly stated. Thus the boundedness and formalness of organizations lends significantly to much a priori knowledge concerning roles and statuses. As such, organizational theory, in combination with prior knowledge concerning roles and positions, can guide the informant selection process.

An important aid in the selection of informants in organizations and other settings is what Miles and Huberman (1984) refer to as a "display." A display is simply a device that provides for the systematic representation of information in a spatial format. Such a formal display often takes the form of a matrix. Other similar examples include Schwartzman's (1983) matrix of communication contexts used in an ethnography of a day-care center. One example from my work in Alaska was an analysis of the range, access, and types of information available to a participant observer in an "active" role in a salmon fish camp (Johnson, 1982). Although originally intended for an understanding of field researchers' roles, the analysis is equally applicable to the selection of informants. Table 3.1 shows an analysis of certain aspects of social roles with respect to such things as ability to interact with members of other roles, access to information, and power within the organization. Both ethnographic observations and prior theoretical knowledge concerning, for example, the organization of work can help in constructing such a display. In this case, assessments of information types and power within the organization were determined to some degree by features of the organization of work. Such things as task diversity, technical interdependence, control over the work pace, technical demands, risk, danger, and uncertainty were seen as important theoretical determinants. For example, high-status positions are characterized as having high levels of skill, less repetition, and minimal amounts of machine pacing, with a work environment involving a high degree of integration and interdependence (Blau, 1964). Other cells were determined through observation; for example, social mobility was determined by how often members of social roles were seen mixing among themselves and with others. Any number of other kinds of frameworks could be constructed, whether they are based on some typology or some other means for identifying the range of categories from which to sample informants.

This is not to say that formal or functional factors should be the only basis for choosing a representative sample of informants. There is increasing evidence that informal networks and relations are important for understanding organizational behavior. For example, Krackhardt and Kilduff (1990) point to the importance of informal social interactions in understanding the emergence and modification of organizational cultures. In another study, Krackhardt (1990) illustrates how an actor's understanding of informal networks affects power within the organization. Boster et al. (1987) found that variations in knowledge of the organization were a function of both formal status and position within an informal network. Thus more emergent or informal methods may be useful in discovering important categories from which to select representative informants. Moreover, the combined use of displays and, for example, informal networks may provide chances for better coverage within and across organizations and other research settings. These matters will be examined more closely in Chapter 4.

The following examples, both in this chapter and the next, have similar formats. In each illustration, the goals, objectives, and hypotheses are described in order to provide a sense of the types of theoretical frameworks employed and the specific factors underlying informant choice criteria. In addition, the specific methods used to select informants are discussed and highlighted. The examples in this chapter are intended to show the application of a more theory-driven framework. As these examples will demonstrate, however, frameworks are not necessarily strictly one or the other, but rather may involve elements of both, in varying degrees, for determining criteria 1 considerations. We start with research that exemplifies most strongly a framework based on a priori assumptions.

Table 3.1 *Characteristics of Social Roles Within the Fish Camp Based on the Organization of Work*

Definable Social Role	Ability to Interact with Other Roles	Access to Information	Accessibility to Organization Sectors	Power Within the Organization	Basis of Power
Boat captain	low	localized, detailed, and limited	low	moderately high	skill and capital investment
Crew	low	localized, limited	low	moderately high	skill and hard work
Carpenter	high	diverse	high	moderately high	skill, technical know-how, and control of resources
Head port engineer	moderate	diverse	high	moderately high	skill, technical know-how, and control of resources
Cook	moderate	diverse	moderately high	moderate	skill and control of resources
Office manager	moderate	localized, detailed, and limited	low	high	skill and control of files and resources
Head carpenter	moderate	diverse	moderate	high	skill, technical know-how, and control of resources
"Beach gang"	high	diverse	high	moderate	ability to perform favors
Superintendent	low	localized, detailed, and limited	low	very high	decision-making status
Port engineer	high	diverse	high	high	skill, technical know-how, and control of resources
Gopher	high	diverse	moderately high	moderately high	control of resources
Tenderworker	low	limited	very low	very low	limited
Night watchman	high	diverse	low	low	limited
Bookkeeper	moderate	moderate	moderate	moderate	control of resources

Example A:
Informant Selection and the Case Cluster Method

McClintock et al. (1983) were interested in applying the underlying logic of survey methods to qualitative case studies involving organizations. In doing so, they were concerned with identifying theoretically representative informants who could be used to elicit units of analysis. This work had a methodological focus and described three examples in which informants provided information on planning events, choice situations, and task identifications within organizations of various types.

BACKGROUND: GOALS, OBJECTIVES, HYPOTHESES

The central theme or argument is that the sampling of informants, and ultimately the units of analysis, should be replicable and unbiased. Bias can be controlled through the selection of informants and units of analysis using theoretical guidance. Such guidance is important for determining sample strata and case clusters for both informants and units, as would be the case in probability sampling involving stratification and clustering. An important feature of the case cluster method, according to McClintock et al. (1983), is that the analytical framework for the case study should be clearly articulated in advance. Ex post facto analytical guides should not be used. This, they believe, facilitates general comparisons across cases and allows for insights as to the relative frequency of events.

INFORMANT KNOWLEDGE OF
PLANNING, CHOICES, AND TASKS

In each of the three examples, McClintock et al. (1983) sought informants who were knowledgeable, motivated, articulate, and accurate. Expectations concerning informants' knowledge were determined on the basis of a priori theoretical considerations (i.e., concern for both criteria 1 and criteria 2). Their first example explored approaches to planning within public sector organizations. Selection was determined through a stratified sample of agencies, informants, and units of analysis involving multiple cases. The underlying rationale for stratification was "based on a theoretical model of organizational planning and on the structure of the human service planning and delivering system" (p. 153). Informants chosen on this basis aided in enumerating "processes that functionally served as planning events" (p. 153). Particular organizational roles from which informants were chosen

UNITS OF ANALYSIS
Type of Choice Situation

Type of Informant	Managerial	Service Delivery
Income maintenance		
Services		
Administration		

Figure 3.1   Stratified Sampling Design for Informants and Choice Situations
SOURCE: McClintock et al. (1983, p. 163).

included planners, managers, and externals. Planners were involved in the direct preparation of planning output. Managers were the ones who "consumed the products of planning" (p. 153). Externals were basically third parties who occasionally observed the planning/consumption process or who interacted with planners or managers in some way.

In the second example, McClintock et al. (1983) wished to test the generalizability of some decision-making theories within a public welfare agency context (e.g., Cohen, March, & Olsen, 1972). In this case, informants were selected on the basis of their position within functional units of the agency. As before, informants were used to enumerate units of analysis, which, in this case, were choice situations (e.g., what action to take as a result of an interview). The three general categories of functional units from which informants were selected included income maintenance, services, and administration. These included mostly supervisory personnel from each. Figure 3.1 shows the sampling design as it relates to the units of analysis.

The third example involved the study of how tasks vary within an organization in terms of complexity and predictability. The sample of informants was stratified on the basis of job classification. The researcher elicited descriptions of tasks from informants that were neither too specific nor too general (e.g., budgeting, typing). The categories from which informants were selected included administrative, faculty, nonfaculty professional, and clerical/maintenance. Job categories were to be compared on the basis of complexity, predictability, and the distribution of task uncertainty.

46

DISCUSSION

This is an excellent example of a theory-driven framework. The categories from which informants were chosen were based on theoretical concerns, such as theories of organizational planning. One of the major advantages of this approach, as seen by McClintock et al., is that case clustering and the quantitative measurement of dimensions facilitate systematic comparisons with other cases. They see this as a means for addressing the external validity problems normally associated with case studies of this kind. In addition, such a procedure has the advantage of being replicable and unbiased (i.e., from a theoretical standpoint). Just how these methods were used in producing the findings of the studies associated with these three examples is difficult to judge. This is because most of the citations that refer to the original studies are either unpublished manuscripts or published abstracts.

Example B:
Key Informants in the Study of Poverty

This example represents the more typical application of the key informant technique in an ethnography involving a multimethod approach. Unlike the next example, which uses survey data as a guide for the selection of informants, in this case key informants were used to help select communities for study and to construct a survey instrument. This example is based on work by Tremblay (1957) on poverty, which was discussed in part in Chapter 2. In this section, I go beyond a discussion of Tremblay's criteria for selecting informants and look in more detail at his actual selection of key informants on the basis of these criteria.

BACKGROUND: GOALS, OBJECTIVES, HYPOTHESES

Tremblay's original study, on which the 1957 article on the key informant technique was based, concerned poverty in Stirling County. A major component of his research was a large survey. In order to ensure the valid and proper selection of communities and relevant questions, Tremblay sought key informants to aid him in the early phases of the research. As mentioned in Chapter 2, key informants could provide folk definitions of poverty and wealth and help in determining the relative poorness of communities and their "true" boundaries.

Preliminary selection of key informants was based on more formal criteria, such as position within the county's political structure and the amount of knowledge or information an informant would have concerning the economic conditions within the county. First, a preliminary list of roles fitting this requirement was constructed and the numbers of individuals in the county within those roles were identified. These formal roles included "bankers, large-scale employers, local government and welfare personnel, as well as such roles as those of newspaper reporters and doctors" (p. 694). Second, because the county was split into two dissimilar municipalities, equal numbers of informants were to be selected for the roles found in both. This represented the preliminary design for the selection of key informants.

Once in the field, Tremblay deviated from the original design for a number of reasons. First, he found that some roles overlapped; for example, some who owned saw mills were also municipal counselors. In this case, only one interview would be conducted instead of the two required in the original design. Many were eliminated due to their general lack of relevant knowledge. In addition, those informants who were highly knowledgeable were consulted more frequently, thus limiting contact with some informants from the original list. As one might expect, the personalities of some individuals inhibited the forming of relationships between fieldworkers and informants. Others were not interviewed because of problems of access (two bankers needed permission from corporate headquarters). Finally, other informants were added at the suggestion of previous informants.

Table 3.2 shows the roles and deviations from the original design. As is evident from the table, a large number of new roles were added during the course of the fieldwork. Thus the selection of informants, although originally guided by prior assumptions, could be altered in light of new evidence or information.

> In brief, the selection of informants was not based on representativeness of age, sex, and locality of residence. The latter would have been important if these individuals had been randomly selected respondents rather than judgmentally selected key informants. The selection was based almost exclusively on intensive knowledge of many communities in the county and ability to impart that knowledge to the interviewer. The symmetrical design was of great utility in maximizing the chances of locating individuals who combined a high degree of knowledge with the ability to communicate it accurately. In short, it was a device for finding "good" informants by first looking into the formal roles which they were likely to occupy. (p. 696)

Table 3.2 *Deviation from the Design in Key Informant Interviewing*

Roles	Number in Design	Number Interviewed
Municipal councillors	21	6
Municipal wardens	2	2
Municipal clerks	2	2
Municipal reporters	2	1
Sawmill owners and cooperative managers	8	6
Doctors and welfare officers	12	7
Bankers	5	2
Farmers	0	3
Legislative Assembly member	0	2
Electric power superintendent	0	1
Tax collector	0	1
Store owner	0	1
Fisherman	0	1
Priest	0	1
Fish plant owner	0	1
Salesman	0	1
School inspector	0	1
Agronomist	0	1
Garage owner	0	1
Total (19 roles)	52	41[a]

SOURCE: Reproduced by permission of the American Anthropological Association from Tremblay (1957, p. 695). Not for further reproduction.

a. Altogether, there were 28 key informants who occupied a total of 41 major economic roles. The difference between the two numbers results from duplicate roles.

It is interesting to note that each key informant was presented with a map as a visual aid and asked "to consider the communities he knew best, and to rate them on a continuum of material wealth" (Tremblay, 1957, p. 696). After examining the map, the informant was asked to point out both the poorest and richest communities, and to give reasons for the responses. Subsequent inquiries prompted informants to move downward from the wealthiest and upward from the poorest, eventually coming to an "average." In the course of these in-depth interviews, informants' responses and reasons were recorded through extensive note taking.

DISCUSSION

What is important about this study is that it is an early example of an important concern for the selection of informants on the basis of their roles and abilities. Tremblay was clearly aware of issues of reliability and validity and provided a clearly stated strategy for the selection of informants. Whether his method covered a representative set of possible informants is unclear. Nevertheless, the information collected with use of key informants made for a more valid and meaningful study, particularly in terms of the survey research. In addition, the study's explicit concern for choice criteria would facilitate both comparability and replication.

This also exemplifies a compromise between theory-driven and emergent frameworks. Whereas a set of roles was determined in advance for selection based on who would likely be most knowledgeable, in practice, selection strategies changed in light of new data. Overlapping roles and the discovery of other knowledgeable roles through, for example, informants' recommendations changed the final makeup of the group of informants used.

The larger study on which this methodological paper was based was conducted by Cornell University in collaboration with the Department of Public Health of the Province of Nova Scotia. The conclusions of the research are not included in the Tremblay article, but in his concluding remarks he states:

> At a later date we hope to publish the results of this validity check for the technique described in this paper, and to set forth some comparisons of results achieved with this and with other research tools in the course of our study. (p. 698)

I was not able to find any of the future work referred to in the methods paper, however.

Example C:
Standardized Indices and the Selection of Informants

The heterogeneity afforded by complex societies has taxed some of the traditional methods of ethnography that have been used in the study of relatively small, homogeneous communities. Robbins et al. (1969) were concerned about the "viability" of these traditional methods in the study of complex societies. In their paper, they discuss the usefulness of survey and statistical analysis in the pursuit of representative, in-depth ethnographic data.

BACKGROUND: GOALS, OBJECTIVES, HYPOTHESES

Robbins et al. (1969) felt that the variation and complexity inherent in larger social systems threatened traditional anthropological approaches. The problem was partly a matter of the selection of reliable and representative informants or cases (e.g., households). They sought a technique that could guide the ethnographer in selecting such cases.

The study focused on cultural identity, acculturation, and modernization among the Baganda of East Africa. The authors were "impressed" by the variations in modernization among members of various communities. People who were Western educated and owned automobiles lived in close proximity to others who lived in traditional houses and wore traditional clothing.

The survey aspect of the research consisted of a sample of 109 households selected at random from six rural villages within a single parish. The survey instrument included questions that sought (a) census and demographic information and (b) indices of acculturation and modernization.

ACCULTURATION AND SELECTION

A variety of questions were used that would discriminate among cases on the basis of the extent of acculturation. A total of 80 variables were selected that concerned exposure to and adoption of Western ideals and values as well as ownership of Western material goods. These dichotomous variables were intercorrelated (phi-correlation coefficients) producing an 80×80 matrix amenable to principal components analysis. Principal components analysis is used to summarize the (mathematical) redundancies among the 80 variables, in effect creating a few summary variables. These resulting indices, or factors, consist of linearly related sets of the original variables. A single variable's contribution to a factor is indicated by its factor loading. The importance of each factor is determined by the amount of variance explained (or its eigenvalue). The distinct advantage of this and other similar techniques is that it allows one to view complex interrelationships among a set of variables in just a few dimensions.

Table 3.3 represents the results of the Robbins et al. (1969, p. 231) analysis showing the first factor. As is evident, the first factor is an indication of acculturation. Variables that correlate (load) highly on this factor,

Table 3.3 *First Factor from Principal Components Analysis*

<table>
<tr><td colspan="4" align="center">*Factor 1*
Variables and Loading</td></tr>
<tr><td>Reads magazines</td><td>.70</td><td>Speaks language other than
Luganda or English</td><td>.43</td></tr>
<tr><td>Banks</td><td>.69</td><td></td><td></td></tr>
<tr><td>House had concrete floor</td><td>.67</td><td>Education greater than 9 years</td><td>.43</td></tr>
<tr><td>Reads English</td><td>.67</td><td>*Kanzu* (native grown) not
worn all of the time</td><td>.42</td></tr>
<tr><td>Speaks English</td><td>.62</td><td></td><td></td></tr>
<tr><td>Drinks European beer</td><td>.61</td><td>Has more than two porters</td><td>.40</td></tr>
<tr><td>Prefers modern drinks</td><td>.61</td><td>Been to Mbarara</td><td>.39</td></tr>
<tr><td>House has concrete walls</td><td>.59</td><td>Prefers drinking from glass
rather than gourd</td><td>.39</td></tr>
<tr><td>Owns stove</td><td>.56</td><td></td><td></td></tr>
<tr><td>Over 40 years of age</td><td>-.56</td><td>Spouse's education between 4
and 8 years</td><td>.38</td></tr>
<tr><td>Owns radio</td><td>.55</td><td></td><td></td></tr>
<tr><td>Prefers distilled drinks</td><td>.54</td><td>Main building roof is metal or
tile</td><td>.34</td></tr>
<tr><td>Western jobs</td><td>.51</td><td></td><td></td></tr>
<tr><td>Owns iron</td><td>.50</td><td>Expanded family</td><td>.34</td></tr>
<tr><td>Reads *Luganda*</td><td>.49</td><td>Spouses's
occupation — Western</td><td>.34</td></tr>
<tr><td>Education 4 to 8 years</td><td>.49</td><td></td><td></td></tr>
<tr><td>Husband and wife eat together</td><td>.45</td><td>Education of spouse more
than 9 years</td><td>.34</td></tr>
<tr><td>Straightens hair</td><td>.45</td><td></td><td></td></tr>
<tr><td>Main house had more than
four rooms</td><td>.45</td><td>Been to Kampala</td><td>.33</td></tr>
<tr><td></td><td></td><td>Drinks banana beer</td><td>-.32</td></tr>
<tr><td>Occupation — Western</td><td>.44</td><td>Been out of the country</td><td>.31</td></tr>
<tr><td>Reads language other than
Luganda or English</td><td>.44</td><td>Owns bicycle</td><td>.31</td></tr>
<tr><td></td><td></td><td>Non-Christian</td><td>.31</td></tr>
<tr><td>Building other than main
house has metal or tile roof</td><td>.43</td><td>Self-identification traditional</td><td>-.31</td></tr>
<tr><td></td><td></td><td>Spouse 40 years or more</td><td>-.31</td></tr>
</table>

SOURCE: Adapted from Robbins et al. (1969, p. 231).

such as read magazines, speak or read English, and prefer modern drinks can all be considered a function of Western influence. The second factor (not shown), on the other hand, is an indication of social marginality, since the features of this dimension include having an atomistic family, not married, preferring "hard" drinks and drinking traditional alcoholic beverages, and not having much in terms of material possessions. Further factors were not presented because they explained very little of the remaining variance.

Individual cases can also be examined in terms of their scores on each of the factors. This provides the basis for Robbins et al.'s selection of representative informants. Thus those with high scores on the acculturation dimension would be cases that have clearly been influenced by Western culture.

Table 3.4 *Scores and Rankings for Six Selected Cases on Factor 1*

Case	Factor 1	
	Score	Rank
52	15.6835	1
10	15.4945	2
8	14.5842	3
9	−0.8190	107
70	−0.9760	108
92	−2.1782	109

SOURCE: Adapted from Robbins et al. (1969, p. 232).

Those cases having low scores on this dimension would consists of households that have generally clung to practices that are more traditional. Cases can be ranked on the basis of these scores, indicating households ranking, for example, from most to least acculturated.

Table 3.4 shows the scores and rankings of the top three and bottom three cases in terms of the first factor of acculturation. Robbins et al. (1969) describe the second-highest-ranked case this way:

> A relatively high *exposure* to Western culture manifested in formal education. The male household head was college-educated although his wife has only a primary school education (6 years). Of the couple's 13 children, 11 have had secondary education or are currently enrolled. The two youngest children are in primary school. High exposure to Western culture patterns is also indicated by the possession of a short-wave radio and the regular reading of *Taifa* and the *Uganda Argus* newspapers (all members of the household read both *Luganda* and English). *Access* to Euro-American culture, or the wherewithal to participate in Western patterns, is also clearly evident. For example the household head possesses a large land-holding and formerly was a high-placed government official. A concomitantly high monetary income permits the payment of school fees for his children, employment of several immigrant tenant farmers, and the purchase of Western material items. He is also familiar with modern techniques of monetary use, such as banking. *Identification* with Western culture is evident in many ways. Perhaps most conspicuous is the possession of a large modern house made of concrete and tile and equipped with electricity. Other notable traits include a preference by female household personnel for straightening hair, a rejection of traditional beverages such as banana beer coupled with a stated preference for European beer, sherry, etc. They also belong to the Church of Uganda, which forbids such traditional customs as polygyny, dancing, and drinking. (p. 232)

While the above is an example of the extreme of acculturation, the following is a description of the lowest-ranking case:

> In this household we have a 68-year-old female living by herself who digs her own garden. She has never been to school and neither reads nor writes *Luganda* or English. Her low income precludes employment of porters or banking, both indications of low economic access to the material attributes of Euro-American culture. This respondent's traditional identification is overtly manifested by residence in a round thatched house and by her preference for unstraightened hair and banana beer. When asked, she identified herself as a "traditional" person rather than a "modern European" type African or "mixture." (p. 232)

Thus informants, at least in this application, can be identified in terms of the extent to which they display features of acculturation, where acculturation is determined inductively through the use of principal components analysis. Cases can all be understood relative to one another and informants can be chosen on the basis of an explicit, replicable procedure.

DISCUSSION

Robbins et al. (1969) discuss several advantages to this method. They note that the use of cases in helping to clarify or define a factor may be ambiguous or unclear. In addition, the procedure allows for a test of the external validity of the factors. Another important aspect of this method is that, since there is a relative understanding of the position of cases along a given dimension, informants can be substituted for one another with less fear of loss of representativeness. This may often be the case when informants refuse to help or drop out of a study for reasons beyond the control of the ethnographer (e.g., illness). In addition, the relative understanding of each household's placement along this dimension allows one to choose informants on the basis of criteria 2 factors with less concern for possible bias. Finally, each case could be understood in terms of both statistical and theoretical representativeness, thus allowing an ethnographer to select informants from across the entire range of cases. Therefore, the in-depth information gained from each informant can be understood in light of such representativeness.

This approach has some of the elements of the a priori framework but is actually more similar to some of the more exploratory techniques that are described in Chapter 4, in which pile sorts and their analysis aided in identifying important folk dimensions of contrast among fishermen (e.g., part-time versus full-time). In both this case and the examples that follow, an analysis of the data revealed patterns that could be used in guiding the selection of informants. It should also be noted that any standardized scale, such as acculturation, can be used to discriminate among cases or to identify subgroups. Thus many standard indicators found in sociological surveys, such as socioeconomic status and locus of control, can be used to construct a framework in which individuals can be identified for more in-depth interviewing.

In a separate article, Robbins and Pollnac (1969) report findings on the relationship between drinking patterns and acculturation. They find that increased acculturation corresponds with trends in informal drinking behavior, modern beverage preference, and the elaboration of drinking contexts, as well as other findings. One should note, however, that the methodological paper discussed above is not cited in this piece, and little mention of the use of the qualitative data is made except in reference to their use of observations that were more impressionistic in nature.

Summary

The first two examples above show clearly how an a priori framework can be applied to the purposive sampling of informants. The McClintock et al. study stressed the importance of such a theory-driven framework in promoting the comparability of cases. In this example, guidelines for determining strata (or categories) from which to sample were determined by theory, fixed in advance, and remained fixed through the course of the research. In the Tremblay example, the formal roles from which he intended to select informants were similarly carefully researched and designed in advance. In this case, however, adjustments were made to the original design as new information became available that shed light on the importance of other roles not anticipated in advance. The Robbins et al. example differed to a great degree from the first two, in that the study has a good deal in common with examples in the next chapter. However, I feel that the researchers' prior theoretical concern for acculturation and modernization, combined with the initial use of formal survey methods, warranted its inclusion in this chapter. This study provided an excellent discussion of a rationale for informant selection on the basis of contrastive features along a single dimension (i.e., index of acculturation).

I would like to make one final observation about these three examples. In each case, the article was presented as a methods piece, with little elaboration on the substantive findings of the relevant research. This is not necessarily unusual, in that there is an apparent failure among many methods papers to link the proposed methods to substantive findings or theoretical debates. The point is that it is difficult to assess the particular contributions of any method to the research process unless one has knowledge of how such methods aided in producing substantive findings. Although such a linkage was generally lacking in these examples, I feel the value of the methods discussed warranted their inclusion.

4. SELECTION BASED ON AN EMERGENT FRAMEWORK

This chapter turns to examples utilizing a more emergent or data-driven framework in the selection of informants. Some of the factors recognized as important bases for the selection of informants in Chapter 2 concerned an individual's status, position, or reputation in a group, society, or culture. In this chapter, several examples of selection procedures based on these concerns are presented. In particular, this chapter provides illustrations of the applications of social network and reputational methods for the selection of informants in the study of commercial fishing villages, elite women in the United States, and food consumption patterns in a midwestern U.S. community.

Informants and Marginality: An Important Lesson

The uniqueness of my first major fieldwork did not prepare me for some of the problems of informant selection I would experience in subsequent field research. My role as both boat carpenter and participant observer in a fish camp in Bristol Bay, Alaska, gave me easy access to a wide variety of potential informants. In particular, my role as carpenter was highly valued in the camp, and all fishermen, from the best to the worst, always had time to talk or to answer questions, or were willing to perform systematic data collection tasks (Johnson, 1982). In graduate school, I had heard horror stories about ethnographers becoming associated with "marginal" informants upon entry into the field. The warning was to be cautious about individuals who try to befriend you in the field; they may be deviants or marginals (Agar, 1980).

In my first major bit of field research after Bristol Bay, I made an extra effort to ensure that my initial informant in the community I was to study (a North Carolina fishing community) would not be deviant or marginal. I contacted the local marine extension agent and asked for his guidance in selecting an entry point into the community. This agent gladly gave me the name of a fisherman he knew well and whom he used regularly for important demonstration projects. I felt confident that my rationale for the selection of this initial informant was well informed.

This initial contact was extremely open and friendly and was more than happy to provide me with the information I requested. However, as I began to spend more time in the community and as I started collecting more kinds of systematic data, it became clear that, in spite of my careful planning, my initial informant was a nothing like William Whyte's Doc in Cornerville.

Figure 4.1 is a multidimensional scaling of a sample (i.e., of resident license holders) of fishermen's aggregated unconstrained judged similarity (derived from a pile sort) of commercial license holders in the community. This technique will be explained in more detail in later examples in this section. Briefly, this figure shows the perceived similarity among commercial license holders. Scalings can be viewed in terms of proximities (i.e., close together in the picture means individuals are alike in some way; far apart, different) or dimensionality (Kruskal & Wish, 1978). A major dimension in this configuration moves from left to right. On the left side are fishermen who were discovered during the course of the ethnographic work to be full-time fishermen (triangles), while those on the right were part-time or retired (squares). The large square denotes the perceived proximity of my initial informant relative to the other license holders. This informant was far outside the group in the community that was most central to my research.

The reasons for this individual's marginal status became apparent over time. First, he was a Yankee in a southern town. Second, he had a pension from the Navy. Such extraneous income often leads other fishermen to perceive its recipient as not being a serious fisherman (Johnson & Orbach, in press). Third, he was a major Republican activist in a mostly Democratic village. Finally, he kept his boat in an isolated anchorage, far from the community harbor.

Fortunately, my initial interaction with this informant did not jeopardize any part of the study. This incident did, however, produce some positive outcomes. I discovered the usefulness of the pile sort technique, both for

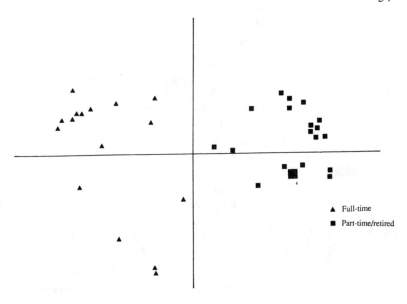

Figure 4.1   Scaling of Fishermen's Perceptions of Community Organization

understanding social organization and as a means for selecting both samples and informants. As an aside, these techniques were also made known to the marine extension agents in the state of North Carolina and nationally. It is just as important for them to utilize systematic procedures in the selection of fishermen for demonstration projects as it is for an ethnographer in the selection of informants (Johnson & Murray, 1989).

Social Networks: A Brief Introduction

The concept of a social network is important for much of what is discussed in this chapter. Social networks can be defined as the webs of social relations established and maintained by individuals in the course of everyday life (Mitchell, 1967). I prefer to think of social networks as sets of social relations that can be represented in a variety of ways (e.g., narratively, conceptually, in matrices or graphs). Much of what will be presented in this chapter will view these networks in both a conceptual and an operational manner.

The more formal definition of *social network* allows for the representation of a network in matrix form. What follows is a simple example of a

Actor
1 0 1 1 1 1 1 0 0 0 0
2 1 0 0 0 0 0 0 0 0 0
3 1 0 0 1 0 0 1 0 0 0
4 1 0 1 0 1 0 0 0 0 0
5 1 0 0 1 0 1 0 0 0 0
6 1 0 0 0 1 0 0 0 0 0
7 0 0 1 0 0 0 0 1 0 1
8 0 0 0 0 0 0 1 0 1 1
9 0 0 0 0 0 0 0 1 0 1
10 0 0 0 0 0 0 1 1 1 0

Figure 4.2   10 × 10 Binary Matrix Showing the Hypothetical Relations Among
Ten Actors

hypothetical social network represented as a binary, chooser-chosen matrix
and two useful relational measures that have been used as proxies for
determining an individual's influence, power, or brokering ability. These
attributes are all important in viewing an individual's access to and control
over information.

Figure 4.2 is a 10 × 10 binary matrix showing the hypothetical relations
among ten actors. For the sake of simplicity, let us say these are friendship
relations, although we could have used other kinds of relations (e.g., co-
workers, advisers). Rows of the matrix provide information on each row
actor's *(i)* friendship choice of a column actor *(j)*. The presence of a link
between two actors i and j is denoted by a 1, while absence of a link is
denoted by a 0. In this hypothetical example, all relations are reciprocal,
leading to a symmetrical matrix. It should be pointed out that relations are
not always reciprocal, and this, in and of itself, is an interesting feature of a
network of relations. For matters of simplicity, all relations will be considered reciprocal in this example.

Binary relations in this matrix can also be represented as a directed or
undirected graph. Since all relations in this example are reciprocal, we will
represent these relations as an undirected graph (i.e., indicate no direction of
choice). Figure 4.3 shows these relations in graph form. The points in the
graph represent each of the ten actors and are termed *nodes*. Lines between
nodes indicate the presence of friendship links and are termed *edges* of the
graph.

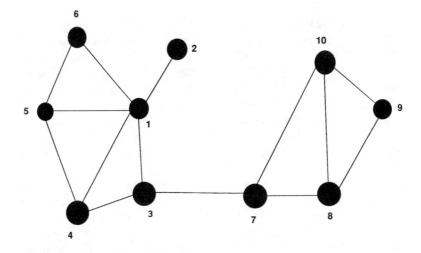

Figure 4.3   Undirected Graph Showing the Hypothetical Relations Among Ten
Actors

A simple visual inspection of the graph shows variations in the number
and kind of links an individual actor maintains. First, in terms of kind, it is
clear that there are two clusters of points or individual actors. Most often
referred to as cliques or subgroups, these spheres of activity have important
implications for behavior. Second, and in terms of number, there are differences among these ten in the number of links connecting them to others.
Actor 1 is the most "active" of the ten actors in the hypothetical network,
having links with five other individuals. This could represent his or her
popularity, control over resources, or power over others. Although not as
central as 1, two other actors have important attributes. Both actors 3 and 7
act as conduits between two distinct cliques. These two have what is referred to as *betweenness* and have implications for power through brokering
information, knowledge, and so on between the two subgroups. In addition,
either actor is in a position to have knowledge concerning the activities of
either subgroup. As we shall see, this has important implications for the
selection of informants in that the establishment of a single informant relationship can provide an efficient means for getting information concerning

the activities of multiple other cliques or actors or information about the members within them.

Often the visual representation of network relations in a graph can be confusing or overwhelming due to complexity or the sheer numbers of actors. Thus cliques become difficult to identify easily by eye, and brokers are not so easily recognized. In such cases we must rely on summary measures that capture these subgroup and relational attributes. There are a large number of graph-theoretic, algebraic, clustering, and factor-analytic techniques for determining subgroups and cliques in network data. Some of these techniques will be illustrated in later sections of this chapter. For now, we will concentrate on the related measures of centrality (activity) and betweenness (brokering).

There have been a number of different algorithms presented for the identification of central actors (Freeman, 1979). For our purposes, we will examine only two. These are simply *point centrality* and *betweenness centrality*. Point centrality is the easiest of the two and refers simply to the linkages (edges in a graph) to or from a single actor. Table 4.1 shows the centrality and betweenness scores for actors in this hypothetical example. Thus actor 1's point centrality in this case is 5, the number of links to others, or, in relative terms, .56 (i.e., proportional to the size of the network).

Betweenness centrality is less straightforward. Conceptually, this form of centrality refers to the extent to which a single node is between or links other clusters of nodes or areas of activity in a network. In this hypothetical example, actors 3 and 7 link two clusters or cliques, thus leading to high betweenness scores. Betweenness has been associated with brokering and power within a network (Freeman et al., 1979). These measures can alert the ethnographer to potentially important informants, particularly in larger, more complex systems of actors. Currently available technology and software allow for the use of these techniques in field situations. Much of the software used to calculate these scores, and to perform the other types of analyses in this section, are available for microcomputers and will run on most lap-top computers.[1]

The examples in this chapter demonstrate the use of a primarily data-driven framework. Once again, however, it should be noted that elements of both frameworks can be combined in establishing the theoretical qualifications of informants. As we shall see, a priori theoretical concerns may guide the informant selection process in earlier portions of the sample, while more emergent criteria guide subsequent selection. The first study in this chapter

Table 4.1 *Centrality and Betweenness Scores for Ten Hypothetical Actors*

	1	2	3	4	5	6	7	8	9	10
Point centrality	0.56	0.11	0.33	0.33	0.33	0.22	0.33	0.33	0.22	0.33
Betweenness	0.44	0.00	0.56	0.07	0.01	0.00	0.50	0.10	0.00	0.10

best exemplifies this in its simultaneous concern for both a priori and emergent criteria in research on elites.

Example D:
Class Consciousness Among Upper-Class Women

Ostrander (1980) provides an example of the selection of informants on the basis of the "snowballing" or referral method in her study of class consciousness among upper-class women in the United States. This study of upper-class women follows in the tradition of elite research best illustrated by the work of Domhoff (1970).

BACKGROUND: GOALS, OBJECTIVES, HYPOTHESES

Ostrander (1980), based on some of her earlier work, believed that the current state of theory concerning class consciousness was inadequate. It was her aim "to critique existing conceptualization of class consciousness using data from interviews with women of the upper class as empirical illustration" (p. 73). To achieve this goal, she conducted an "inductive" study involving in-depth focused interviews among upper-class women in a midwestern city. She used emergent nondirective questioning, in which additional questions may be added or old questions changed in light of new evidence. Thus data drove the direction of her theoretical investigation.

The study involved interviews with 38 upper-class women. According to Ostrander (1980):

> The sample of respondents was obtained by asking each woman at the conclusion of the interview if she would suggest "another woman of your social group, with a background like yours, who might be willing to talk to me." The initial respondent who set off this "snowball" method was located largely by accident, though she met the objective criteria I had established. A colleague who knew of my study and had worked with this woman on a community project suggested that I contact her. She was immediately enthusiastic about my interest in "learning about the role of women in some of the old and

influential families in the city." She offered to refer me to the oldest "grandes dames," who would give me further entrée. She said, "It's important for you to go in the right order. You have to start at the top." I had so little difficulty gaining the consent of my subjects to be interviewed and taped that my experience leads me to conclude that upper-class persons are more accessible than has been previously thought, and I urge my fellow social scientists to be less hesitant in approaching them. (p. 75)

The selection of the first respondent, or "seed," was guided by theory found in the literature as recognized by Ostrander (Baltzel, 1958; Dahl, 1961; Domhoff, 1970). The particular features of this initial respondent, and all subsequent referrals, included the following: membership in upper-class clubs and the Junior League; intergenerational attendance in class-designated, private secondary schools; graduation from elite colleges (Smith, Vassar, Wellesley); listings in the *Social Register*; husbands in key positions in business; many presidents of boards or chairs, with some heading prestigious, well-established family businesses; husbands in law or medicine if not in business; and clear social linkages to the first families or firms of the city (Ostrander, 1980). Thus features pointed out in the literature as important indicators of the upper class were used as selection criteria for the initial seed. It is interesting to note that subsequent referrals fit these criteria equally well.

DISCUSSION

This example is particularly illustrative of the importance of referrals in gaining access to informants. More important, Ostrander was fortunate enough to have an initial informant point out the importance of the "right order" of moving from top to bottom. Under these conditions, each successive referral would come from a woman of greater or equal status. These top-to-bottom referrals would have certainly aided in establishing the legitimacy of her work. Ironically, it may have been the very phenomenon that Ostrander was studying—class or status consciousness—that helped her move in a seemingly effortless manner through this group of upper-class women.

In terms of analytical frameworks, this example has aspects that can be considered both data driven and theory driven. The initial selection of informants was guided by what previous research and theory said about women of the upper class. Subsequent selection was based on snowballing, a more data-driven procedure for selection.

These informant interviews helped Ostrander in concluding that activities (e.g., debuts) and their associated meanings are what ultimately reflect class consciousness. She sees class consciousness as a function of activities or behaviors within the class context. Thus "women of the upper class are highly 'class conscious' because they behave in ways dictated by the social object of class in everyday life" (p. 94). She viewed her in-depth emergent methods as the proper means for the study of such phenomena, particularly across different contexts.

Example E:
Social Networks and Innovation Adoption

There has been a considerable amount of research in the social sciences on the diffusion of innovations. This has resulted in a bewildering array of hypotheses, with an equally bewildering number of studies displaying conflicting findings (Johnson, 1986; Rogers & Kincaid, 1981; Rogers & Shoemaker, 1971). Most of the earlier research employed survey techniques in which the dependent variable, adoption, was related to a number of independent variables, generally characteristics of the adopters (e.g., age, income), in one or several regression models.

I attempted to avoid the pitfalls of these more traditional atomistic approaches by conducting a study of the influences of social relations on adoption behavior through both the quantitative and ethnographic study of social networks (Johnson, 1986). The study consisted of an ethnographic investigation of a small fishing village in eastern North Carolina. The diffusion of two important technological innovations through the community of fishermen was the focus of the study.

BACKGROUND: GOALS, OBJECTIVES, HYPOTHESES

The overall objective of the study was to understand the influences of the network of social relations on the adoption of innovations. An underlying theoretical assumption is that adoption cannot be understood solely through an investigation of the attributes of actors—attributes that are not necessarily reflective of social interaction (e.g., income, education). Rather, adoption behavior is better understood through an investigation of the influences actors exert on one another toward rejection or adoption of any technology. More specifically, I wanted to test the hypothesis that two structurally equivalent actors will adopt an innovation at approximately the same time. The term *structural equivalence* refers to the extent to which two actors in a network share overlapping relations. Thus the more that two individuals have the same communication relations, for example, the more the two are structurally equivalent (Burt, 1982; Johnson, 1986). Such an approach to the study of the diffusion of innovations is important because it allows for a systematic investigation of important sociological concepts, such as normative action (Johnson, 1986). The selection of key informants in this study was crucial for understanding the nature of adopting new technologies and the role of network subgroupings in the adoption process.

UNDERSTANDING THE NETWORK OF RELATIONS

Methodologically, the study required the complete mapping of the network of social relations for active fishermen in the fishing village. Unlike many studies of this type, the potential universe of fishermen involved in the diffusion process was known. Commercial fishermen are required to obtain licenses from the state; thus the names of fishermen who reported Crab Town (pseudonym) as their place of residence could be obtained from the North Carolina Division of Marine Fisheries.

The total number of licenses issued to residents of Crab Town was larger than the probable universe of full-time fishermen that would be involved in any diffusion process. The pile sort technique, discussed earlier in this chapter, provided an assessment of the activeness of license holders in the community. In this case, the technique involved presenting informants with cards containing the names of fishermen licensed in the community, which will be referred to as *stimuli*. Informants were asked to sort the names into piles according to how similar they perceived those individuals to be to one another. They could have as many or as few piles as they wished. Following the completion of the task, informants were asked to explain their sorting behavior. (Example E in this chapter provides an illustration of the forms and kinds of reasoning fishermen used in the course of sorting.)

These *similarity judgments* could then be aggregated across informants in the form of a similarity matrix. The data in this form were then amenable to a number of factor-analytic techniques that can spatially represent perceived social relations, such as multidimensional scaling. A more in-depth explanation of the sorting procedure and construction of the similarity matrix can be found in Weller and Romney (1988). A good explanation of multidimensional scaling can be found in Kruskal and Wish (1978).

Since this procedure is employed early in the ethnographic enterprise, it is not obvious who should be selected for the administration of this type of task. The most important consideration for selection of informants at this early stage should be the general grasp of knowledge they have concerning other members of the community. Individuals who are themselves stimuli (i.e., listed) can be approached. Less knowledgeable informants will be unable to recognize names or will have difficulty classifying individuals. Those less informative informants can be dropped from any aggregation, leaving just those who appear more knowledgeable (e.g., knowledgeable informants are those who have the smallest "don't know" pile). More knowledgeable informants' responses can be aggregated and subjected to analysis, as in this example, or can be informative simply on the basis of their ethnographic content, as will be demonstrated in Example F.

In this case, the pile sort data can be aggregated and scaled in order to reveal the structure of the similarities among licensed fishermen. Thus all fishermen on the left side of the configuration in Figure 4.1 are active full-time fishermen. This group provided the initial list from which to begin the network and ethnographic interviewing.

Fishermen for this final list were contacted and interviewed and were asked to provide information on their networks (e.g., who one interacts with frequently and who one talks to frequently on the radio). In addition, fishermen were asked to name others they thought were "smart" and "experimenters." These two concepts were found earlier in the study to be folk indicators of a fisherman's ability.

Figure 4.4 provides an analysis of the network data (e.g., based on frequency of interaction) showing sets of structurally equivalent fishermen as determined using cluster analysis. A discussion of the methods for such an analysis can be found in Burt (1982) and Johnson (1986). What is important to understand here is that these network subgroupings corresponded almost precisely with folk classifications of different fishing groups as described by informants. The cluster marked S4 was termed by informants the "little fleet" and contained fishermen in their late teens and early 20s. The cluster designated S3 was called the "big fleet" and contained fishermen mostly in their late 20s or early 30s. The other two groups consisted of two brothers, one of whom was considered the best fisherman in the community (S1), and larger group with less clear patterns of interaction, some members of which were related through kinship (S2).

This figure is presented to illustrate the nature of relations among the fishermen of this community. Such an analysis was conducted after the study was completed, and was not used in the formal selection of key informants. However, it is important to point out that with advancements in

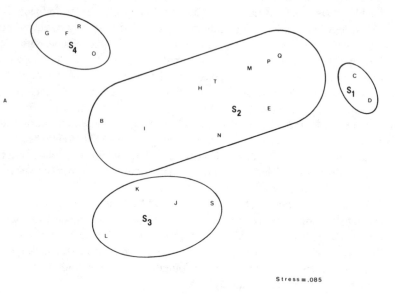

Stress = .085

Figure 4.4   Scaling of Distance Matrix and Identification of Structurally Equivalent Actors with Clustering

microcomputer technology and the availability of appropriate software, it is now considerably easier to conduct many kinds of preliminary analysis in the field. Nevertheless, an informal analysis of the raw network data was used to help select key informants.

Based on an informal analysis of frequencies of citations in terms of relations, rankings of smartness and experimentalism, and informal observations, key informants were selected on the basis of subgroup membership, status within the subgroup, linkages between groups, and overall status in the community. Thus it was clear that more in-depth ethnographic interviews would need to be conducted with one or more members of the little fleet and the big fleet. In addition, fisherman D, who received the largest number of citations, both in terms of social relations and in terms of smartness or experimentalism, would need to be interviewed in more depth.

Based on this less formal analysis, fishermen P, D, G, and S were selected as key informants, and the ethnographers (two of whom were involved in the actual collection of data) participated in shrimping aboard these informants' fishing vessels. In addition, fisherman S was selected as a key informant not only for his membership in the big fleet, but also because of his links to other groups (i.e., high betweenness) and his high rankings in terms of smartness and being an experimenter. The same is true for fisherman D, who was considered the best fisherman in the community.[2]

Selecting informants in this manner provided access to all segments of the social system. Since many of the social network subgroupings were based on radio communication behavior, fishing with active members of these groups allowed for the monitoring of other vessels as well. In addition, fishermen who ranked high, in terms of both social activity (e.g., centrality) and fishing ability (i.e., rated as smart and experimenters), tended to be extremely knowledgeable about the technological innovations that were the focus of the study.

In addition, a more formal analysis (not shown) of network centrality scores discussed earlier for each of the fishermen in the network was conducted. Our informal analysis in the field corresponded well with the more formal analysis. For example, fisherman D, a major informant, was high in terms of both measures of centrality. Fisherman G, who was selected as an informant from the little fleet, had the highest point centrality score from that subgroup. A major informant from the big fleet, fisherman S, had the highest combined centrality score outside of fisherman L for the group. He also ranked high on both the smart and experimenter dimensions. In addition, his moderately high betweenness was a result of his links to D. Whereas fisherman L had the highest combined scores of any in the network, his links were primarily to the younger fishermen of S4 (plus A and B) as well as to his own subgroup. In addition, he ranked lower in terms of being an experimenter or smart. It is often the case that betweenness alone is not the most important factor. Often it is important also to take into consideration the nature of the links that contribute to the brokering position.

DISCUSSION

An important aspect of the methods described above is their multiwave, emergent character. Depending on the focus of the study, a large group of potential interest can be reduced to a significantly smaller, more manageable size through the use of the pile sort procedure. This reduced set of actors can then be studied more closely in terms of the informal relations among actors so that social groupings can be discovered and active participants in such groupings identified. At this level, informants can be selected on the basis of, for example, their control over group activities (e.g., community leaders), subgroup membership, or their brokering characteristics between two or more subgroups. The precise selection, of course, will depend on the nature of the study. Thus, in this case, selection across network subgroups is the important basis for selection, whereas selection across categories or along dimensions of contrast might be important in some other study.

The pile sort technique has some important advantages, particularly in a field setting, and is similar to the projective aids discussed in Chapter 2. The technique has been administered in bunkhouses, on fishing boats, in informants' houses, on piers, and in municipal buildings. In literate societies, blank 3 × 5 cards can be quickly transformed into stimuli with the names of individuals, households, kin groups, or any other domain of material typed or written on the front. In nonliterate societies, Polaroid pictures can be used in an analogous manner. Once again, pictures of people, houses, chiefs, and so on are equally feasible, depending on the nature of the investigation. Classification of stimuli can be either *constrained* or *unconstrained*. Constrained pile sorts can involve ranking or classification based on set criteria (e.g., clan membership). Another important aspect of such a task relates to informants' explanations for their sorting behavior. Such explanations are often rich in ethnographic detail. The general usefulness of pile sorts has been discussed in more detail elsewhere (Weller & Romney, 1988). However, this technique's use as a means for understanding the characteristics of potential informants, particularly key informants, has only recently been explored.

In sum, this study found that structural equivalence tended to account well for adoption behavior. The ethnography, in which the informants played an important role, helped in determining needed adjustments (e.g., exponent values) to the mathematical model of equivalence. Thus the qualitative component of the study provided insight into the proper specification of quantitative parameters.

Example F:
The Organization of Fishing in the Florida Keys

In a study by Johnson, Orbach, and Waters (1987), a multimethod approach was used to explore the potential social and economic impacts of limited entry — an exclusionary resource management tool — on the spiny lobster fishermen of southern Florida. The study involved a research team in which a simple random sample, a stratified random sample, and a corresponding survey instrument were used to understand the general characteristics of the population of spiny lobster fishermen in the Florida Keys. A more detailed description of this aspect of the research can be found in Johnson and Orbach (in press) and Holbert and Johnson (1989). A major component of the research design of this study involved ethnography of two communities in the Florida Keys. One ethnography focused specifically on Cuban fishermen in the Key West area (Cruz, 1987). The second focused on a community of fishermen outside the two major fishing ports of Marathon and Key West. The first was conducted to ensure a better understanding of ethnic participation in the fishery, while the second was performed to gain an understanding of the "independent" fishermen who fish from the backs of their houses.

In this example, we will focus on the community of "independent" fishermen, which will be referred to as the Pine Torch Key (pseudonym) community (Johnson & Orbach, in press). Similar to the previous example, a combination pile sort and network approach was used.

BACKGROUND: GOALS, OBJECTIVES, HYPOTHESES

The primary objective of the large study (Johnson et al., 1987) was to determine the potential social and economic impacts of limited entry on the participants of the southern Florida spiny lobster fishery. A second component of the study focused on the effects of urbanization on the organization of commercial fishing (Johnson & Orbach, in press), specifically focusing on the impacts of zoning, leisure and tourism industries, and increasing social stratification on the commercial fishermen of the area.

An interesting element of this study was the social stratification among the fishermen, which was based on differences in class, income, occupational commitment, and ownership of commercially zoned fishing property. As any researcher who has investigated any economic enterprise in the United States or elsewhere will admit, many respondents or informants are reluctant to disclose economic information. Even in the event of disclosure, the validity of the data is often questionable. In this case, key informants were critically important for providing validity checks on the spectrum of economic information gained in the sample. This is in addition to the kinds and types of information afforded by "knowledgeable" fishermen from the various subgroups on fishing locations, effort, catch rates, and other important elements of the fishing operation that are often proprietary.

PILE SORT AND SNOWBALL SAMPLE

Similar to Example E above, the list of individuals with commercial licenses residing in the Pine Torch Key community was obtained from the Florida Department of Natural Resources. Names were typed on 3 x 5 cards and coded for identification. In this particular application of the technique, the pile sort data themselves were used to identify the core fishermen in the community. This core could then become the initial wave in a snowball sample through the community (Johnson, Boster, & Holbert, 1989).

The pile sort was administered to a small number of fishermen. Initially, a commercial fisherman recognized by the Organized Fishermen of Florida (who additionally was selected in the primary random sample as important, because he was past president of the organization) was administered the pile sort task. In the course of completing the task, he provided additional names not previously identified and identified individuals who were inactive or not known. Sortings were noted and the explanations for the sortings recorded on tape. Based on this informant's recommendations, a second "knowledgeable" fisherman was contacted and given the pile sort task. Once again, sortings were noted and the interview recorded.

It may be instructive to present the types of responses provided in the course of the interviews. Upon completion of the pile sort task, informants were asked to give reasons for placing names together in piles. The following are examples of explanations for piles given by the first two informants: "don't know"; "They are either in some other business full- or part-time — definitely not people who fish for a living"; "These are legitimate, serious fishermen that get the bulk of their income from fishing"; "He has two sons who he opened up a gym with — he goes fishing on the good days and doesn't get but 25 or 30% of his income from fishing"; "He has been in a number of businesses, but just started fishing 100%"; "He's a great guy who is a sheriff's deputy that fishes on weekends"; "These guys are not a whole lot dependent on fishing"; "claims to be a fisherman"; "a fishing family"; and "big fishermen who handle a lot of fish."

It is clear from these explanations for the groupings that there are a variety of kinds of fishermen as perceived by the informants. Such data, particularly when aggregated across a number of informants, provide a good indication of just what constitutes the "core" and "periphery," at least as perceived by the fishermen themselves.

On the basis of the two initial interviews, it became apparent which license holders were inactive, which were part-time commercial fishermen, and which were full-time commercial fishermen. Two more interviews were conducted to help confirm the reliability of these earlier interviews. The second set of interviews did not differ in content in any major way from the first two. Based on these groupings from the four interviews, a core list of full-time commercial fishermen was constructed to be used in the initial wave of a snowball sample.

Fishermen from this core list ($n = 10$) were contacted and interviewed using a survey instrument constructed for the larger study. At the end of the questionnaire, respondents were asked to name five fishermen they talked to frequently about commercial fishing. After fishermen from the core list had been interviewed, the five people each had cited were subsequently contacted and interviewed, if they had not already been interviewed. The sample stopped when new names mentioned were those of fishermen who did not live in Pine Torch Key.

This resulted in a snowball sample of the commercial fishermen of Pine Torch Key. The co-citation data resulting from the sample could be represented as a binary chooser-chosen matrix. Data in this form are amenable to a number of analytical and graphic techniques commonly employed by social network analysts, as discussed earlier. Johnson and Orbach (in press) subjected this matrix to correspondence analysis, which has the capability of representing relationships among both rows and columns of an asymmetric or symmetric contingency table or any $n \times m$ matrix in low-dimensional space (e.g., two-dimensional Euclidian space). Correspondence analysis can be viewed as a descriptive or exploratory method that summarizes relatively complex numerical information into a spatial configuration (Weller & Romney, in press). Figure 4.5 is an analysis of the rows of this chooser-chosen matrix. Similar to the example above, subgroups consisting of sets of structurally equivalent actors are determined with the use of average-linkage clustering.

As is evident from Figure 4.5, there are four subgroupings based on the patterns of social interaction among these 28 fishermen. The subgroup termed S_1 consists primarily of an older, "gentrified" group of fishermen

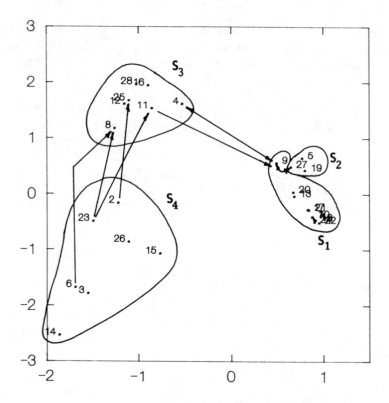

Figure 4.5   Correspondence Analysis of Rows (Choices) of Binary Matrix with
Status/Role Sets, Structurally Equivalent Actors Identified and Links
Between Subgroups Shown

who tend to have income extraneous to commercial fishing. Subgroup 2 (S_2) consists of relatively younger fishermen who fish from the same neighborhood as members of S1. Subgroup 3 (S_3) contains fishermen who are the most active in the fishermen's organization as well as two of the most highly respected fishermen in the community. Subgroup 4 (S_4) contains a mixture of young and old fishermen, most of whom had moved to the Keys within a ten-year period.

Once again, an attempt was made to establish relationships with key informants from each of the groupings. The two most respected and active fishermen, 11 and 28 from S_3, were selected for their extensive knowledge of the community and the fishery as a whole. One of the single most important key informants selected was fisherman 9. As Figure 4.5 also shows, this fisherman had links (the arrows) across several subgroups and was perceived as a hardworking, knowledgeable fisherman, even for someone who was so young. This fisherman became an important source of validation for a variety of different types of economic data, particularly concerning the members of S_1, a group of "gentrified" fishermen who were extremely interesting from a socioeconomic and class standpoint.[3] This fisherman was contacted for periodic updates even after the completion of the research. In a formal analysis of the binary network data, fisherman 9 had one of the highest combined centrality scores as well as *the* highest betweenness centrality in the network.

DISCUSSION

This example is similar to the previous one in terms of its emergent character. In addition, the flexibility of the pile sort procedure was demonstrated once again. The procedure was used to facilitate discussions of relations among individuals in an ethnographically informative manner. It was also useful for initially reducing the potential universe of fishermen to a more manageable size. This reduced universe then provided the basis for additional investigation into the network of relations among the active fishermen in the community (i.e., the snowball sample). Informants could then be chosen on the basis of subgroup membership, reputation, or linkages across subgroups, thereby ensuring strategic coverage across this system of actors.

The selection of an informant based on betweenness was extremely important for checking the validity of responses for a survey instrument. A single informant provided invaluable data on the true economic dependency of a certain subgroup of fishermen. In light of these data, the responses could be corrected, thus improving the theoretical significance of the analysis.

In sum, this study described the factors currently contributing to changes in the spiny lobster fishing industry in southern Florida. One important finding of this study was the importance of social stratification in understanding fishermen's behavior. Although the quantitative network methods helped to identify the groups within this stratified system of actors, the ethnographic component aided in checking the validity of information that ultimately determined the basis for such stratification. Without these key informant interviews, the quantitative analysis would certainly have been less meaningful.

Example G:
Understanding Consumer Behavior

A study by Griffith, Johnson, and Murray (1988) provides another example of the use of snowball sampling for the selection of informants. Methodologically, the study involved a multimethod approach including probability sampling, the administration of questionnaires and pile sort tasks, and an ethnographic component. The ethnographic component supplements the survey by providing richer information on the influence of social context on the phenomenon under study.

The study was regional in scope and included a phone survey methodology that involved a stratified random sample of inland and coastal rural and urban residents. An important aspect of the study was the ethnographic investigation of a moderate-sized inland community. It is this portion of the study that is the focus of the discussion below.

BACKGROUND: GOALS, OBJECTIVES, HYPOTHESES

The research objectives relevant to the issues described here were (a) the examination of the effects of varying levels of knowledge on consumers' perceptions of seafoods relative to other foods (e.g., poultry, beef, canned meats), and (b) an assessment of the interactions of social networks, knowledge of seafood, learning, and consumption in both coastal and inland populations. An important element of the ethnographic study, the use of a snowball sample, is that it allows for an investigation of the influence of social context and relations on both the distribution of knowledge concerning seafood and seafood consumption patterns themselves. This type of investigation fills a gap left by the survey due to its requisite atomistic orientation (i.e., independence of cases; see Coleman, 1958).

In an attempt to achieve these objectives, a small-to-moderate-sized midwestern town was chosen that ranged in population from 10,000–20,000, had an economic base not solely dependent on agriculture, and was sufficiently removed from the influences of an urban or university environment (all factors found in a pilot study to influence consumption). A small town fitting these criteria was chosen: Moberly, Missouri. Located approximately in the center of the state, Moberly has a population of approximately 13,451 and has a relatively varied industrial base that includes, for example, the production of chemicals and automobile parts.

The initial phase of the community ethnography involved informal interviews of informants with expertise on the character of the town. These included city employees, most notably building inspectors (code enforcement officers), and local real estate agents. Unlike ethnographic research in non-Western settings, where the collection of original census data and the construction of maps are essential aspects/components of early research, such data were available through both public and private sources. Thus zoning maps were available through city hall, and adequate street maps could be obtained from the Chamber of Commerce or through real estate offices. In addition, census information was available from county, state, and national sources.

Early interviews with city employees and real estate agents consisted of "walks" through the city during which these "expert" informants were asked to point out features of the town, particularly any discernible or notable neighborhood boundaries based on ethnicity or social class. Questions about the cost of housing in certain areas and the "eliteness" of certain areas aided in the acquisition of such information.

Earlier research on seafood consumption (Griffith & Johnson, 1988) pointed to the influence of income on patterns of consumption. Therefore, it was necessary to initiate the interviewing in a "middle-class" neighborhood, since there is strong evidence that lack of seafood consumption for lower-middle-class and low-income households is largely a function of income. Based on the initial ethnographic methods described above, a neighborhood was selected that is relatively homogeneous in terms of the socioeconomic status of its residents. Thus the "Meadowbrook" neighborhood was chosen for the initial seed interview.

SNOWBALL SAMPLE AND INTERVIEWS

Streets in the Meadowbrook neighborhood were assigned numbers. One street was chosen at random, and the houses on or adjacent to the street were assigned numbers. Once again, a number was chosen at random, and a house near that area fitting the following criterion was chosen: The household had to have some indication of containing children. (Randomness was not necessary for this particular method, but was used here to help narrow down the large number of potential seeds or initial choices.) This precaution was largely to ensure that a household of retired individuals was not the initial seed in the sample. Griffith and Johnson (1988), in some preliminary research, found the elderly were more fixed in their consumption patterns, being less influenced by factors such as social relations, point-of-purchase advertising, and so on.[4] Thus avoiding households containing older residents would ensure that the initial seed and subsequent citations would be households that had higher probabilities of displaying variations in consumption patterns. The initial seed household for the Meadowbrook neighborhood is represented by a 1 in the lower right-hand portion of Figure 4.6.

The interviews consisted of three phases, during which the interviewee went from playing the role of subject to being a respondent to being an informant. The entire interview consisted of the administration of a pile sorting task, followed by a survey instrument, ending with a series of semistructured questions concerning diet and recent changes in diet.

In the middle of the survey, respondents were asked to provide the names of three individuals or households with whom they interacted on a regular basis. This formed the basis for the snowball sample. Figure 4.6 shows the geographical distribution of the 30 informants.

The squares (seed 2) and triangles (seed 1) in the figure represent informants obtained from two distinct seeds (samples). The selection of a second seed was necessary due to the direction (in terms of SES) of subsequent households based on the initial seed. An explanation of the underlying rationale for the selection of a second seed will help illustrate the unique flexibility afforded by this method.

Household 1 (lower right), the initial seed, was chosen because of its location (i.e., middle-classness) and household composition (i.e., containing children). However, the first of the three citations to be interviewed was household 2, which was located in an area of the city where household incomes were much lower, on average, than those found in the Meadowbrook neighborhood. Subsequent citations revealed other households in the lower- to middle-income range. The sample based on the initial seed moved through households with relatively lower incomes but also households containing more elderly individuals. An advantage to this method is that after only a few interviews of related informants, patterns can be observed and documented and future sample points can be chosen that send the ethnographer into yet unexplored areas. This is similar to the idea of theoretical saturation (Glaser & Strauss, 1967). Thus, after patterns began to reveal themselves following several interviews with informants from seed 1, it was decided to initiate a second, parallel sample containing middle- to upper-middle-income households.

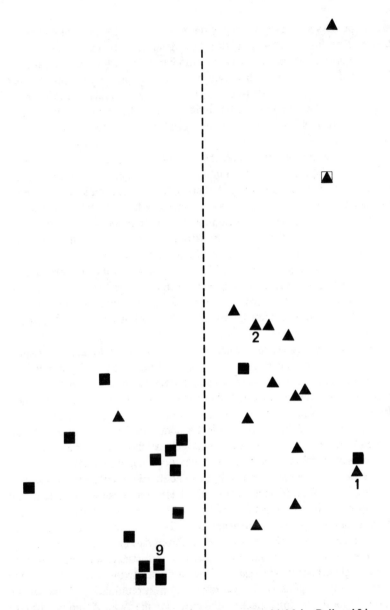

Figure 4.6 Geographical Distribution of Informants, with Major Railroad Line Through Town Shown

In a process similar to the selection of seed 1, seed 2 (household 9) was chosen from an "elite" neighborhood (as determined by expert informants, including real estate agents and code enforcement people), and once again a household was chosen that had evidence of containing children (a swing set was seen in the backyard). This household was asked to name three households, and so on. The snowball sample based on this second seed is represented by squares in Figure 4.6, while those from the first are represented by triangles.

As can be seen in the figure, the overall distribution of sample points varies with respect to each original seed. That is, most triangles are on the right, while most squares are on the left. What this distribution illustrates is that social relations in this town are somewhat a function of which "side of the tracks" one lives on. The geographical dividing line between these two seed clusters is the main railroad track running north and south through the city (represented in the figure by the dashed line).

This division was also evident in an examination of the network data. A sociogram (not shown) of relations among members of the two seeds illustrated how the snowball sample of informants provided us with in-depth data from two distinct areas of town, in terms of both residence and social interaction.

For the purposes of the consumer behavior study, these interviews provided for both quantitative and qualitative data. Of particular importance were the semistructured ethnographic interviews, which attempted to document dietary changes and informants' perceived reasons for these changes. But what is of greatest benefit, particularly from a theoretical standpoint, is the fact that these interviews could be understood in relation to a better understanding of the potential influences of social context on behavior (i.e., the roles of social interaction, church, country club, and so on).

A second aspect of the research involved interviews with experts to help in identifying folk distinctions of class based on housing. Pictures of the houses of all of the 30 informants were taken, numbered on the back for identification, and encased in clear plastic. These represented a set of stimuli to be given to experts for unconstrained classification.

Expert informants in this case had to be individuals who were familiar with neighborhoods and housing in the city. The obvious individuals in this case were the experts who were relied upon in preliminary phases of the research for describing aspects of the city, as in the "walks" through the city discussed earlier. These included real estate agents and code enforcement officers (i.e., building inspectors). Six expert informants were chosen, including four real estate agents and two code enforcement officers. One real estate agent was chosen from each of four major real estate offices in town. The two code enforcement officers represented the total universe for such a distinction in the city government.

Informants were asked to examine the pictures and then sort them into piles according to how similar they perceived the houses to be to one another. Following this task, informants were asked to explain their sorting behavior. These explanations, although structured, often led to other relevant informal discussions about housing and other socioeconomic concerns in the city. Such explanations and any subsequent questions were recorded.

It is interesting to note that the stimuli, pictures, are a natural part of the occupational world of both real estate agents and code enforcement officers. This was brought to my attention in the course of the interview with the second expert, a real estate agent for a large, nationally known firm. Upon completion of the sorting and explanation, the informant reached into his desk drawer and produced a large stack of pictures that he had taken of houses. These pictures were used in presentations to customers and for real estate listings books. Similarly, a code enforcement officer brought out pictures of houses showing code violations. In both cases, the sorting task was approached with more ease and less confusion than I have ever seen before. Thus, among these experts, the particular method employed was extremely "natural."

Figure 4.7 is a multidimensional scaling of the aggregated judged similarity data of informants' houses by the experts with clusters, determined with average linkage clustering, encompassed by circles. Note that members of the two samples tend to share membership in clusters. Cluster 1 contains the wealthiest of the second sample, who tend to reside in large, new homes in an elite neighborhood, while cluster 5 and, to some extent, cluster 2 contain the more upwardly mobile in this sample who live in nice, older homes. This analysis also informs us of the division by socioeconomic status within the first sample. Those in cluster 3 tend to have nicer homes than those in cluster 4. This method may be useful for finding informants' representativeness based on certain class distinctions as determined with the use of the expert informants. These distinctions or categories provide further criteria on which to base selection for more in-depth interviews and investigations.

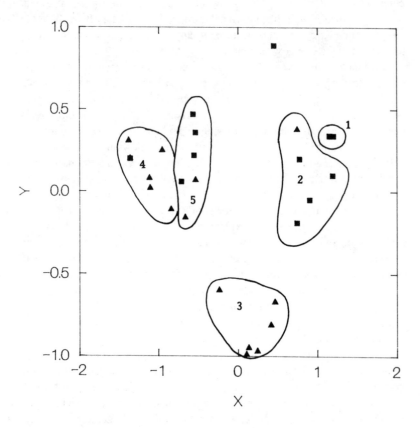

Figure 4.7   Multidimensional Scaling of Judged Similarity of Informants' Houses

DISCUSSION

This example uses elements of both theory- and data-driven frameworks. The two seeds were chosen on the basis of important theoretical criteria as determined by earlier research. Subsequently, "snowballing" was more of an emergent process in the discovery of informants, as was the sorting of informants' households by experts.

The methods described have a number of important advantages, in terms of both meeting the needs of data collection in the field and providing the proper criteria for comparability or partial replication. First, it is often difficult to begin a community study, particularly with respect to the collection of qualitative data. The snowball procedure provides the ethnographer with the explicit means for moving through the community in some methodologically and theoretically meaningful way. The ethnographer can easily keep track of the interview process (Werner, 1989). Social relations among members of the community can be understood on the basis of class, ethnicity, income, religion, and so on. An understanding of these relations can provide opportunities for the selection of key informants based on position in the community, location in a neighborhood, or any particular influences an individual may have over others (e.g., a particularly active church member).

Second, and similar to the earlier example, informants can be chosen on the basis of their informal brokering characteristics (e.g., linkages with different groups) or their central position within a group or the community as a whole. For example, two informants were found to link the two separate seed samples. These individuals could provide valuable information concerning factors linking socioeconomically distinct groups within a community (e.g., religion).

Third, the referral aspects of this technique can provide credibility and better accessibility to other informants. During the early phases of the research, I was initially greeted with suspicion and, sometimes, hostility by potential informants. I was quite perplexed by this behavior since I was working in a relatively moderate-sized midwestern town. The only other time I had experienced anything remotely similar was during some research in urban Miami, Florida. I later discovered that an article had been published in the local paper about a month prior to my arrival warning local residents to beware of the con tactics of door-to-door and phone salespeople. Some of my informants told me that they had initially thought I was trying to sell "groceries." One informant, in fact, said that "he had taken this same survey before" and "didn't want to buy any groceries."

I did eventually interview this informant and his family, but only after gaining an understanding of his social world and the referral of his church's minister. In another case, an elderly widow stated she had opened her door only because I had mentioned the name of one of her best friends, a former informant. The technique proved to be invaluable under these conditions for gaining access to informants. Eventually, people were calling ahead and informing others of my imminent arrival. I would often be greeted at the door and would be jokingly referred to as "the fish man."

Finally, the procedure provides opportunities for replication and comparability. Other ethnographers using similar theoretical assumptions and methods should be able to test related hypotheses in the same or similar communities.

In preliminary analysis of these data, Johnson and Boster (1990) found that class has an important influence on the perception of similarities among various meats. Informal interviews with informants helped in identifying the institutional bases for the establishment and maintenance of social relations, also important considerations in accounting for variability in perception. The social context of interaction in the lower-class sample was the church, while for the upper-class sample it was the country club. Food was a peripheral aspect of interaction among members of the first sample, while food was a central aspect of social interaction among members of the second (i.e., they ate meals with one another frequently). Thus food was much more salient in class-related social interactions among members of the upper-class sample.

Summary

The four examples presented in this chapter illustrate a balance between the applications of theory- and data-driven frameworks. Initial parameters for selection in each case were determined on theoretical grounds, and subsequent choices were based on the emergent properties of the data. In the study of elites, the initial informant was selected on the basis of characteristics that were viewed as theoretically important. Further informants were then chosen through the referral or snowball procedure. In both the Crab Town and Pine Torch Key studies, a multistage method was used in which names on the official list of fishery participants (e.g., state license lists) were presented to local informants (chosen from those listed) for assessment (i.e., pile sort). Subsequent interviews were based on these assessments through either a complete interviewing of participants or a snowballing procedure. Key informants in each case could then be selected on the basis of subgroup membership and relational attributes (e.g., centrality), thus ensuring strategic coverage across subgroups within this system of actors. The final example also incorporated a snowball procedure, but, as in the elite study, the initial selection of seeds was based on factors considered to be of theoretical concern to the study at hand (e.g., socioeconomic status).

NOTES

1. Centrality scores were calculated using the network analysis package UCINET.

2. Fishermen B and K were also used as key informants in terms of the ethnographers participating aboard their vessels.

3. This is an example of a case where a question yielded perfect reliability with no validity. The question, "What percent of your income is derived from commercial fishing?" yielded a 100% response from all of the "gentrified" fishermen. It was clear, however, that many of these fishermen had pensions and investment income. Fisherman 9 was included in cross-validating the responses from the questionnaire.

4. One exception often involves the loss of a spouse. In addition, health concerns have played an important role in the changing diets of the elderly.

5. A LOOK AHEAD

This final chapter has two purposes. First, the cultural consensus model (Romney et al., 1986) alluded to earlier is examined more closely in terms of its potential usefulness in the selection of informants. The model's recent introduction has limited its widespread application, thus we look ahead by exploring its potential applications for the selection of informants. Second, some brief concluding remarks are provided that draw together the preceding chapters in terms of selection criteria.

New Concerns: Knowledge and Selection

In Chapter 2 we briefly touched upon the idea that variation in knowledge (e.g., cultural knowledge) has important implications for the selection of informants. Some have pointed out that such variation is evidence that viewing culture as what is shared is "unproductive" (Gardner, 1976). In defending the idea that culture is shared (Werner & Fenton, 1970) or is a mean around which there is variation (D'Andrade, 1970), Boster (1985, 1986) studied variation in Aguaruna knowledge of manioc, an important crop. He found a single model of manioc identification and that variation within the model was a function of the sexual division of labor, membership in kin and residential groups, and individual expertise. As he notes, this work has important implications for informant selection:

> One implication of this work is that the now-maligned practice of using key informants may not be so bad after all. In the case of Aguaruna manioc identification, one could pick informants who have more knowledge of the

cultural model than others. These older women approach Werner's ideal of the omniscient informant in that their knowledge of manioc represents a "union of individual competences" (Werner, 1969:333). Deviations from their identifications can be considered mostly the results of either performance errors or ignorance. A careful ethnographer might have chosen these women to interview on the basis of a knowledge of the rest of the society. The problem is that only by studying variation could the ethnographer be assured of having made the right choice. (Boster, 1985, pp. 193-194)

The idea that there exists a single model of cultural knowledge for a given domain and that individual deviation from the model can be determined was formalized by Romney et al. (1986) in their cultural consensus model. This model sees agreement as a reflection of shared knowledge and the fact that some individuals know the cultural system better than others, implying that individual knowledge levels can be estimated from interinformant agreement. Thus a systematic means for assessing the knowledge level or "competence" of informants is available.

Example H: Consensus and Selection

I depart here from the format of earlier examples by demonstrating the usefulness of the cultural consensus model through a hypothetical extension of data from a previous study. Although consensus theory has great potential for aiding in the selection of informants, its recent introduction has limited its widespread application to date. Therefore, we take data on the perception of social structure from a study of a university administration office by Boster et al. (1987), and show how consensus can be applied to the selection of informants in this case.

The original study was interested in examining "the relationship between social position and agreement with others on social structure" (Boster et al., 1987, p. 377). An important portion of the study was concerned with how knowledge of the social structure of the office was distributed. For our purposes, we will assume that knowledge of the social structure is an important basis for informant selection. We want the most competent individuals for informants, where competence is determined by an individual's fit to the consensus.

KNOWLEDGE OF GROUP STRUCTURE

Two primary kinds of data were collected from the 16 members of this administration office. These included unconstrained judgments of similarity among all actors in the office and network data involving two kinds of advice rankings: work advice and personal advice. This discussion will concentrate on the former. Unconstrained similarity judgment was based on both pile sort tasks and triad tests. In the triad test, informants were asked to judge which of three actors was most different from the other two. A balanced incomplete block design (Burton & Nerlove, 1976) was used in which each pair of the 16 actors occurred in exactly two triad sets. The resulting 80 distinct triads were presented to each of the 16 informants in random order. The pile sort task was similar to those discussed in earlier sections. Informants were asked to sort the names of office actors into as many piles as they wished according to which they thought were most similar to one another.

These data on the perceived structure of the group, or proximities among its members, were compiled at both individual and aggregate levels. Similarity matrices for the 16 informants were produced from the judged similarity data. Aggregate similarity matrices were produced by summing across all 16 informants for each of the two procedures. Agreement among actors or knowledge shared among informants on the social structure was determined on the basis of correlations (Pearson's r) between individual similarity matrices. This resulted in two interinformant agreement matrices for the triad test and the pile sort data. For the sake of simplicity, we will focus on the agreement matrix derived from the triad test.

Minimum residual factor analysis was used to solve for individual "competencies." Competence is similar to how well an individual's responses correlate with those of the rest of the group. The interinformant agreement matrix based on the triad test fit the cultural consensus model. As mentioned previously, the model is a formalization of the idea that agreement reflects shared knowledge and that, since some informants can be expected to have more knowledge than others, individual knowledge levels (i.e., competence) can be estimated from interinformant agreement. If the matrix fits the model, there should be a single-factor solution such that there are no negative scores on the first factor and that the first latent root (eigenvalue) should be relatively large in comparison with all other roots. In this case, the triad test data fit the model. There are no negative scores on the first factor and the first latent root is 6.7 times larger than the next latent root.

Table 5.1 *Competency Scores for the 16 Actors*

Actor	Score	Position
1	0.856	professional staff
2	0.625	support staff
3	0.563	support staff
4	0.901	graduate student worker
5	0.830	support staff
6	0.871	support staff
7	0.630	professional staff
8	0.757	graduate student worker
9	0.700	undergraduate worker
10	0.291	undergraduate worker
11	0.775	support staff
12	0.217	undergraduate worker
13	0.689	undergraduate worker
14	0.522	undergraduate worker
15	0.700	professional staff
16	0.895	professional staff

Competence, or knowledge level, as indicated by the model, is shown for each of the 16 actors in the office in Table 5.1. This rank ordering of actors reveals that individual competence or knowledge varies to some extent by virtue of status in the office. Higher-status actors tend to agree with each other more than do lower-status actors. Figure 5.1 shows this graphically. This figure is a multidimensional scaling of the interinformant agreement matrix based on the triad data. Each of the formal statuses in the office is denoted by a symbol: professional staff, circle; support staff, triangle; graduate student worker, box; and undergraduate student worker, diamond. Those actors who agree more or who have a better fit to the consensus are in the middle of the configuration, while those on the periphery tend to agree less.

If we consider competence with respect to knowledge of the social structure (as determined by perceived proximities) to be an important consideration for the selection of informants, then it is clear that some actors in the office would make better informants than would others. Those in the middle of the figure, or who have highest competence/knowledge, would certainly be better than those on the periphery. Thus undergraduate student workers, in this case, would not be the best possible informants for gaining more detailed information on the social structure of the office.

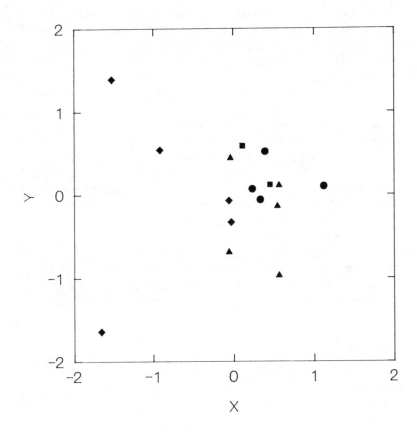

Figure 5.1   Scaling of Interinformant Agreement Matrix

DISCUSSION

This procedure provides some advantages similar to those of the Robbins et al. (1969) example (Example C, in Chapter 3). Individuals can be understood in terms of their relative knowledge or reliability, allowing for the substitution and interchangeability of informants or key informants. Determination of individual competencies facilitates better understanding of potential selection bias due to individuals' variation in knowledge of a cultural domain, thereby ensuring the selection of knowledgeable informants.

With regard to analytical frameworks, this is another good example of a selection method that is emergent. Criteria 1 considerations are determined on the basis of individual approaches to a triad test. It should be noted, however, that this could just as easily have been an approach to a sentence completion task, a true/false test, or a multitude of other means for assessing expertise or competence within a domain of knowledge. The consensus model allows for estimation of individual competencies (or knowledge levels) from interinformant agreement measures. Once relative competencies are known, the researcher can use criteria 2 considerations to direct final selection without fear of introducing bias (e.g., "cooperative" informants with demonstrated knowledge of the culture can be identified and interviewed further). This corresponds to the suggestions of Spradley and McCurdy (1972) that informants should be selected on the basis of their knowledge of the culture as well as a number of criteria 2 considerations.

This analysis can be performed in the field with currently available software on most lap-top computers. A method for determining relative competencies through hand calculations is discussed by Bernard (1988). A more detailed treatment of the consensus model can be found in Romney et al. (1986), Weller and Romney (1988), and Bernard (1988) (e.g., sample sizes, test construction).

Concluding Remarks

The preceding chapters have provided a variety of examples of rationales for the selection of informants in ethnographic research. In each case, there was concern for the theoretical qualifications and representativeness of informants, where such qualifications and representativeness were determined through the use of either theory-driven or data-driven analytical frameworks. In some cases, the determinants for the selection of informants were totally theory driven (e.g., Example A), while in other cases they were primarily emergent or data driven (e.g., Example E). In most cases, however, elements of both played a role in the development of an explicit rationale for the selection of informants.

Once representativeness is understood within a system of actors, the personal attributes of potential informants can play a role in their ultimate selection. Articulateness, willingness to participate, trustworthiness, and other personal attributes then become screening devices. At this point, personal attributes can drive the selection process with less risk of potential bias. However, even among the examples presented in this volume there is still a need for greater detail in the reporting of informant selection procedures and rationales in ethnographic writings. In more quantitatively oriented work, probability sampling designs and rationales are explicitly described. This allows readers to assess the adequacy of designs in terms of their potential for introducing bias of any kind. In addition, such detail facilitates verification efforts. Future ethnographic work should similarly include more discussion and detail regarding justifications for the selection of informants. Descriptions and discussions of nonprobability sampling designs should routinely be included in the general discussions of ethnographic research methods in papers, books, and grant proposals. At the very least, such discussions should be included in detailed notes or appendices. This form of presentation has the benefit of providing the proper specification of methods without disrupting the storytelling nature of the ethnographic product.

In sum, the use of explicit procedures for the selection of informants has clear implications. The better we understand the methods and procedures of other ethnographers, the better our chances are for partial replication or the comparability of research findings. This effort will enhance chances for the further accumulation of knowledge in the social sciences and will help ensure that ethnography and qualitative methods play a more central role in this cumulative enterprise.

REFERENCES

Adler, P. A., & Adler, P. (1987). *Membership roles in field research.* Newbury Park, CA: Sage.

Agar, M. H. (1980). *The professional stranger: An informal introduction to ethnography.* New York: Academic Press.

Arnold, D. O. (1970). Dimensional sampling: An approach for studying a small number of cases. *American Sociologist, 5,* 147-150.

Baltzel, D. (1958). *Philadelphia gentlemen.* New York: Free Press.

Berlin, B., Breedlove, D. E., & Raven, P. H. (1968). Covert categories and folk taxonomies. *American Anthropologist, 70,* 290-299

Bernard, H. R. (1988). *Research methods in cultural anthropology.* Newbury Park, CA: Sage.

Bernard, H. R., & Killworth, P. D. (1977). Informant accuracy in social network data, II. *Human Communications Research, 4,* 3-18.

Bernard, H. R., Killworth, P. D., & Sailer, L. (1980). Informant accuracy in social network data IV: A comparison of clique-level structure in behavioral and cognitive network data. *Social Networks, 2,* 191-218.

Bernard, H. R., Killworth, P. D., & Sailer, L. (1982). Informant accuracy in social network data V: An experimental attempt to predict actual communication from recall data. *Social Science Research, 11,* 30-66.

Bernard, H. R., Killworth, P. D., Sailer, L., & Kronenfeld, D. (1984). On the validity of retrospective data. *Annual Review of Anthropology, 13,* 495-517.

Blau, P. M. (1964). The research progress in the study of the dynamics of bureaucracy. In P. E. Hammond (Ed.), *Sociologists at work.* New York: Basic Books.

Borman, K. M., LeCompt, M. D., & Goetz, J. P. (1986). Ethnographic and qualitative research design and why it doesn't work. *American Behavioral Scientist, 30*(1), 42-57.

Boster, J. S. (1985). Requiem for the omniscient informant: There's life in the old girl yet. In J. Dougherty (Ed.), *Directions in cognitive anthropology.* Urbana: University of Illinois Press.

Boster, J. S. (1986). Exchange of varieties and information between Aguaruna manioc cultivators. *American Anthropologist, 88,* 428-436.

Boster, J. S., & Johnson, J. C. (1989). Form or function: A comparison of expert and novice judgments of similarity among fish. *American Anthropologist, 91*(4), 866-889.

Boster, J. S., Johnson, J. C., & Weller, S. C. (1987). Social position and shared knowledge: Actors' perceptions of status, role, and social structure. *Social Networks, 9,* 375-387.

Brim, J. A., & Spain, D. H. (1974). *Research design in anthropology: Paradigms and pragmatics in the testing of hypotheses.* New York: Holt, Rinehart & Winston.

Burt, R. S. (1982). *Toward a structural theory of action.* New York: Academic Press.

Burton, M., & Nerlove, S. B. (1976). Balanced designs for triads tests: Two examples from English. *Social Science Information, 5,* 247-267.

Campbell, D. T. (1955). The informant in quantitative research. *American Journal of Sociology, 60,* 339-342.

Cohen, M. D., March, J. G., & Olsen, J. P. (1972). A garbage can model of organizational choice. *Administrative Science Quarterly, 17*, 1-25.

Coleman, J. S. (1958). Relational analyses: The study of social organization with survey methods. *Human Organization, 17*, 28-36.

Collier, J. (1957). Anthropology: A report on two experiments. *American Anthropologist, 59*, 843-859.

Cook, T., & Campbell, D. T. (1979). *Quasi-experimentation: Design and analysis for field settings.* Chicago: Rand McNally.

Crawford, M. (1989). Utah looks to Congress for cold fusion cash. *Science, 244*, 522-523.

Cruz, M. (1987). *The Cuban fishermen of Key West.* Unpublished master of arts thesis, Rutgers University.

Dahl, R. A. (1961). *Who governs? Democracy and power in an American city.* New Haven, CT: Yale University Press.

Dalton, M. (1964). Preconceptions and method. In P. E. Hammond (Ed.), *Sociologist at work.* New York: Basic.

D'Andrade, R. G. (1970). *Culture shared and unique.* Paper presented at the annual meetings of the American Anthropological Association.

D'Andrade, R. G. (1976). A propositional analysis of U.S. American beliefs about illness. In K. H. Basso & H. A. Selby (Eds.), *Meaning in anthropology.* Albuquerque: University of New Mexico Press.

Domhoff, G. W. (1970). *The higher circles: The governing class in America.* New York: Random House.

Douglas, J. D. (1976). *Investigative social research.* Beverly Hills, CA: Sage.

Dow, M. (Ed.). (1989). Comparative analysis [Special issue]. *Journal of Quantitative Anthropology, 1*(4).

Fabrega, H., & Manning, P. K. (1972). Health maintenance among Peruvian peasants. *Human Organization, 31*, 243-256.

Fielding, N. G., & Fielding, J. L. (1987). *Linking data.* Newbury Park, CA: Sage.

Freeman, L. C. (1979). Centrality in social networks I: Conceptual clarification. *Social Networks, 1*, 215-239.

Freeman, L. C., Fararo, T. J., Bloomberg, W., Jr., & Sunshine, M. H. (1963). Locating leaders in local communities: A comparison of some alternative approaches. *American Sociological Review, 28*, 791-798.

Freeman, L. C., Roeder, D., & Mulholland, R. (1979). Centrality in social networks II: Experimental results. *Social Networks, 2*, 119-141.

Freeman, L. C., & Romney, A. K. (1987). Words, deeds, and social structure. *Human Organization, 46*, 330-334.

Freeman, L. C., Romney, A. K., & Freeman, S. C. (1987). Cognitive structure and informant accuracy. *American Anthropologist, 89*, 310-325.

Gardner, P. (1976). Birds, words, and a requiem for the omniscient informant. *American Anthropologist, 3*, 446-468.

Garro, L. C. (1986). Intracultural variation in folk medical knowledge: A comparison between curers and noncurers. *American Anthropologist, 88*, 351-370.

Geertz, C. (1973). *The interpretation of cultures: Selected essays.* New York: Basic Books.

Glaser, B. G., & Strauss, A. L. (1967). *The discovery of grounded theory: Strategies for qualitative research.* Chicago: Aldine.

Glass, G. V (1976). Primary, secondary, and meta-analysis of research. *Educational Researcher,* 5, 3-8.

Griffith, D. C., & Johnson, J. C. (1988). *Eat mo' fish: Using anthropology to increase and diversify seafood consumption in the U.S.* Paper presented at the annual meetings of the Society for Applied Anthropology, Tampa, FL, and at Marine Resource Utilization: A Conference on Social Science Issues, Mobile, AL.

Griffith, D. C., Johnson, J. C., & Murray, J. D. (1988). *Social and cultural dimensions among seafood consumers: Implications for consumer education.* Proposal to the University of North Carolina Sea Grant College Program.

Hively, W. (1989). Cold fusion confirmed. *American Scientist, 77,* 327.

Holbert, D., & Johnson, J. C. (1989). Using prior information in fisheries management: A comparison of classical and Bayesian methods for estimating population parameters. *Coastal Management, 17,* 333-347.

Honigmann, J. J. (1970). Sampling in ethnographic fieldwork. In R. Naroll & R. Cohen (Eds.), *Handbook of method in cultural anthropology.* New York: Columbia University Press.

Hunt, R. G. (1970). *Strategic selection: A purposive sampling design for small numbers research, program evaluation, and management.* Buffalo: State University of New York, Survey Research Center.

Jacobs, J. (1977). *Statesville: The penitentiary in mass society.* Chicago: University of Chicago Press.

Jick, T. D. (1983). Mixing qualitative and quantitative methods: Triangulation in action. In J. Van Maanen (Ed.), *Qualitative methodology.* Beverly Hills, CA: Sage.

Johnson, J. C. (1981). *Cultural evolution and the organization of work: Scarcity and resource management in an Alaskan fishery.* Unpublished doctoral dissertation, University of California, Irvine.

Johnson, J. C. (1982). *Of strangers and outsiders: Ethnography and serendipity in coastal communities.* Paper presented at the annual meetings of the American Anthropological Association, Washington, DC.

Johnson, J. C. (1986). Social networks and innovation adoption: A look at Burt's use of structural equivalence. *Social Networks, 8,* 343-364.

Johnson, J. C., & Boster, J. S. (1990). *Of pigs, cows, chickens, and shrimp: Community structure and cognitive variability.* Paper presented at the annual Social Network Conference, San Diego, CA.

Johnson, J. C., Boster, J. S., & Holbert, D. (1989). Estimating relational attributes from snowball samples through simulation. *Social Networks, 11,* 135-158.

Johnson, J. C., & Miller, M. (1986). Behavioral and cognitive data: A note on the multiplexity of network subgroups. *Social Networks, 8,* 65-77.

Johnson, J. C., & Murray, J. D. (1989). *Social structure and technology transfer: Applications in extension.* Paper presented at the annual meeting of the Society for Applied Anthropology, Santa Fe, NM.

Johnson, J. C., & Orbach, M. K. (in press). A fishery in transition: The impact of urbanization on Florida's spiny lobster fishery. *City and Society.*

Johnson, J. C., Orbach, M. K., & Waters, J. (1987). *Limited entry alternatives for the Florida spiny lobster fishery: A preliminary analysis.* Report to the Gulf of Mexico and South Atlantic Fishery Management Councils.

Kempton, W. (1981). *The folk classification of ceramics: A study of cognitive prototypes.* New York: Academic Press.

Killworth, P. D., & Bernard, H. R. (1976). Informant accuracy in social network data. *Human Organization, 35*, 269-286.

Killworth, P. D., & Bernard, H. R. (1979). Informant accuracy in social network data III: A comparison of triadic structures in behavior and cognitive data. *Social Networks, 2*, 19-46.

Kimball, S. T., & Partridge, W. L. (1979). *The craft of community study: Fieldwork dialogue.* Gainesville: University Presses of Florida.

Kirk, J., & Miller, M. L. (1986). *Reliability and validity in qualitative research.* Beverly Hills, CA: Sage.

Krackhardt, D. (1990). Assessing the political landscape: Structure, cognition, and power in organizations. *Administrative Science Quarterly, 35*(2), 342-369.

Krackhardt, D., & Kilduff, M. (1990). Friendship patterns and culture: The control of organizational diversity. *American Anthropologist, 92*, 142-154.

Krenz, C., & Sax, G. (1986). What quantitative research is and why it doesn't work. *American Behavioral Scientist, 30*, 58-69.

Kruskal, J. B., & Wish, M. (1978). *Multidimensional scaling.* Beverly Hills, CA: Sage.

Lastrucci, C. L. (1963). *The scientific approach: Basic principles of the scientific method.* Cambridge, MA: Schenkman.

Manning, P. K., & Fabrega, H., Jr. (1976). Fieldwork and the "new ethnography." *Man: The Journal of the Royal Anthropological Institute, 2*, 39-52.

Marcus, G. E. (1986). Contemporary problems of ethnography in the modern world system. In J. Clifford & G. E. Marcus (Eds.), *Writing culture.* Berkeley: University of California Press.

McClintock, C. C., Brannon, D., & Maynard-Moody, S. (1983). Applying the logic of sample surveys to qualitative case studies: The case cluster method. In J. Van Maanen (Ed.), *Qualitative methodology.* Beverly Hills, CA: Sage.

McCracken, G. (1988). *The long interview.* Newbury Park, CA: Sage.

Mead, M. (1953). National character. In A. L. Kroeber (Ed.), *Anthropology today.* Chicago: University of Chicago Press.

Metzger, D., & Williams, G. E. (1966). Procedures and results in the study of native categories. *American Anthropologist, 68*, 389-407.

Miles, M. B., & Huberman, A. M. (1984). *Qualitative data analysis: A sourcebook of new methods.* Beverly Hills, CA: Sage.

Miller, M. L., & Johnson, J. C. (1981). Hard work and competition in an Alaskan Fishery. *Human Organization, 40*(2), 131-139.

Mitchell, J. C. (1967). On quantification in social anthropology. In A. L. Epstein (Ed.), *The craft of social anthropology* (pp. 17-64). London: Tavistock.

Notes and queries in anthropology. (1951). London: Routledge & Kegan Paul.

Ostrander, S. A. (1980). Upper-class women: Class consciousness as conduct and meaning. In G. W. Domhoff (Ed.), *Power structure research.* Beverly Hills, CA: Sage.

Pelto, P. J., & Pelto, G. H. (1975). Intra-cultural diversity: Some theoretical issues. *American Ethnologist, 2*, 1-18.

Pelto, P. J., & Pelto, G. H. (1979). *Anthropological research: The structure of inquiry.* Cambridge: Cambridge University Press.

Pinxten, R. (1981). Observation in anthropology: Positivism and subjectivism combined. *Communication and Cognition, 14*, 57-83.

Poggie, J. J., Jr. (1972). Toward quality control in key informant data. *Human Organization, 31*, 23-30.

Pollnac, R. B. (1975). Intracultural variability in the structure of the subjective color lexicon in Buganda. *American Ethnologist, 2*(1), 89-109.

Robbins, M. C., & Pollnac, R. B. (1969). Drinking patterns and acculturation in rural Buganda. *American Anthropologist, 71*(2), 276-285.

Robbins, M. C., Williams, A. V., Kilbride, P. L., & Pollnac, R. B. (1969). Factor analysis and case selection in complex societies. *Human Organization, 28,* 227-234.

Rogers, E. M., & Kincaid, D. L. (1981). *Communication networks: Toward a new paradigm for research.* New York: Free Press.

Rogers, E. M., & Shoemaker, F. F. (1971). *Communication of innovations.* New York: Free Press.

Romney, A. K. (1989). Quantitative models, science and cumulative knowledge. *Journal of Quantitative Anthropology, 1*(1/2), 153-223.

Romney, A. K., & Faust, K. (1983). Predicting the structure of a communications network from recalled data. *Social Networks, 4,* 285-304.

Romney, A. K., & Weller, S. C. (1984). Predicting informant accuracy from patterns of recall among individuals. *Social Networks, 4,* 59-77.

Romney, A. K., Weller, S. C., & Batchelder, W. H. (1986). Culture as consensus: A theory of culture and informant accuracy. *American Anthropologist, 88,* 313-338.

Rosenthal, R. (1984). *Meta-analytical procedures for social research.* Beverly Hills, CA: Sage.

Schwartzman, H. (1983). The ethnographic evaluation of human service programs: Guidelines and illustrations. *Anthropology Quarterly, 56,* 179-189.

Scott, W. R. (1965). Field methods in the study of organizations. In J. G. March (Ed.), *Handbook of organizations.* Chicago: Rand McNally.

Seidler, J. (1974). On using informants: A technique for collecting quantitative data and controlling measurement error in organization analysis. *American Sociological Review, 39,* 816-831.

Spindler, G. (1955). *Socio-cultural and psychological process in menomine acculturation.* Berkeley: University of California.

Spradley, J. P., & McCurdy, D. W. (Eds.). (1972). *The cultural experience: Ethnography in complex society.* Chicago: Science Research Associates.

Stake, R., & Easley, J. (Eds.). (1978). *Case studies in science education.* Urbana, IL: Center for Instructional Research and Curriculum Evaluation.

Tremblay, M. (1957). The key informant technique: A non-ethnographical application. *American Anthropologist, 59,* 688-701.

Tyler, S. A. (1969). *Cognitive anthropology.* New York: Holt, Rinehart & Winston.

Van Maanen, J. (Ed.). (1983). *Qualitative methodology.* Beverly Hills, CA: Sage.

Van Maanen, J. (1988). *Tales of the field: On writing ethnography.* Chicago: University of Chicago Press.

Wagley, C. (1983). Learning fieldwork: Guatemala. In R. Lawless, V. H. Sutlive, & M. D. Zamora (Eds.), *Fieldwork: The human experience.* New York: Gordan & Breach.

Waldrop, M. M. (1989). Cold water from Caltech. *Science, 24,* 523.

Warwick, D. P., & Lininger, C. A. (1975). *The sample survey: Theory and practice.* New York: McGraw-Hill.

Weller, S. C., & Romney, A. K. (1988). *Systematic data collection.* Newbury Park, CA: Sage.

Weller, S. C., & Romney, A. K. (in press). *Metric scaling: Correspondence analysis.* Newbury Park, CA: Sage.

Werner, O. (1969). The basic assumptions of ethnoscience. *Semiotica, 1,* 32-338.

Werner, O. (1989). Keeping track of your interviews I. *CAM Newsletter, 1*(1), 6-7.

Werner, O., & Fenton, J. (1970). Method and theory in ethnoscience. In R. Naroll & R. Cohen (Eds.), *Handbook of method in cultural anthropology*. New York: Columbia University Press.

Werner, O., & Schoepfle, G. M. (1987). *Systematic fieldwork* (2 vols.). Newbury Park, CA: Sage.

Whyte, W. F. (1955). *Street corner society: The social structure of an Italian slum*. Chicago: University of Chicago Press.

Whyte, W. F. (1984). *Learning from the field: A guide from experience*. Beverly Hills, CA: Sage.

Young, F. W., & Young, R. C. (1961). Key informant reliability in rural Mexican villages. *Human Organization, 20*, 141-148.

ABOUT THE AUTHOR

JEFFREY C. JOHNSON is an Associate Scientist in the Institute for Coastal and Marine Resources and Associate Professor in the Department of Sociology and Anthropology, East Carolina University. He received his Ph.D. from the University of California at Irvine, where he conducted ethnographic research as a participant observer in a fish camp in Bristol Bay, Alaska. His research interests include the application of quantitative and qualitative methods in ethnographic research, social networks, diffusion models of innovation, small group dynamics, and relationships between social structure and cognition. He has published extensively in sociological, anthropological, and marine journals and is the current editor-in-chief of the *Journal of Quantitative Anthropology.*